THE EDITOR

W. H. Hutchinson of Chico State College in Chico, California, is the author of *A Bar Cross Man*, a biography of Eugene Manlove Rhodes, and he has provided introductions for Rhodes's *Stepsons of Light*, *The Proud Sheriff*, *The Trusty Knaves*, *Copper Streak Trail*, and *Paso por Aquí*, all published by the University of Oklahoma Press.

THE WESTERN FRONTIER LIBRARY

BRANSFORD IN ARCADIA

BRANSFORD IN ARCADIA

or
The Little Eohippus

by
Eugene Manlove Rhodes
with an Introduction by
W. H. Hutchinson

University of Oklahoma Press : Norman

Library of Congress Cataloging in Publication Data
Rhodes, Eugene Manlove, 1869–1934.
    Bransford in Arcadia.
    (The Western frontier library)
    I. Title.
PZ3.R3443Br6   [PS3535.H68]   813'.5'2
74–15905
ISBN 0–8061–1261–1

INTRODUCTION
by W. H. Hutchinson

'Gene Rhodes began work on this novel, here re-printed with its original ending for the first time, late in 1908. After a long gestation, it was serialized in the *Saturday Evening Post*, November 30—December 28, 1912, and brought its author hundreds of fan letters and figurines of horses by the score. In terms of tangible reader response, it was the most successful of all his writings, either in magazine or book form. Several reasons can be advanced for this happy circumstance.

Imprimis, it was a romance crammed with action that spoke deeply to the values and the mores of the upwardly mobile readers whom George Horace Lorimer, the five-button mandarin of the *Post*, was wooing assiduously and successfully for his magazine. It also spoke deeply to the tenor of the Progressive era, when the nation's middle class, the backbone of that era, was torn between fascination with the material benefits of industrialization and nostalgia for a simpler, rural time. Second, none of those who wrought truly about the West-That-Was, with the exception of Charles M. Russell and, possibly, Ross Santee, worked from the "inside-out" as knowledgeably as did Rhodes. Witness the brief passage hereinafter where Jeff Bransford transforms himself from a cowboy cavalier into a hard-rock miner. To one who has worked "down the hole," it is redolent of blast smoke and quartz dust. Rhodes' writing, as well, was "pricked with allusion and sparkling with wit;" it complimented his readers' intelligence and possessed a narrative drive that induced and sustained the willing suspension of disbelief that is the *sine qua non* of fine fiction. Finally, and perhaps most importantly, this was a cowboy story with a difference, a matter that requires some examination here.

Such competent horseback-and-cloister students of the West as Bernard DeVoto, J. Frank Dobie, and Walter Prescott Webb have noted that Owen Wister's *The Virginian* (1902) made the cowboy respectable enough for proper literary attention. Equally skilled in his own right, Wallace Stegner has noted that the collaboration and cross-fertilization between Wister and Frederic Remington prior to 1902 encompasses the ontogeny of the cowboy as a literary figure. It is not intended here to dispute the findings of these archaeological excavations into the storied splendors

of America's vanished Papyrus Age. Neither is it intended to question the fact that *The Virginian* was an
instantaneous book and stage success which made a
very great deal of money for its author, a wholly new
and agreeable Wisterian experience.

It is necessary to note that *The Virginian* caused no
discernible increase in the incidence of cowboy stories
in the quality, general-audience, mass circulation
magazines that heralded the dawning, between 1900–
1910, of the Golden Age of American Popular Fiction
which reached high noon in the years following World
War I. Neither did Wister's creation measureably
alter the image of the cowboy presented to millions of
readers weekly and monthly by these same magazines.
Detailed examinations of *American Magazine*, *Collier's*, *Cosmopolitan*, *Everybody's*, *McClure's*, *Mun-
sey's*, *Red Book* and *Saturday Evening Post* for the
first decade of this century have provided the temerity
to make the preceding statements.

Of these magazines, *Saturday Evening Post* is regarded as the most representative. Its appeal was not
urban-oriented, as was *American's*; it was not aimed
at a specific audience, as *Cosmopolitan* was aimed at
the female seeking psuedo-sophistication; it did not
descend into the lurid exposé, as did *Everybody's*,
and it eschewed the virulent "muckraking" that dis-
tinguished both *Collier's* and *McClure's* during this
period. Withal, the *Post* was far from bland and its
sustained drive for the intelligent conservation and
use of natural resources was a distinguishing dif-

ference. The breadth of its appeal is demonstrated un-equivocally by its upsurge in circulation between 1900–1910.

In this decade, the nation's population increased from 76,000,000 to 92,000,000, while the *Post's* circulation soared from ± 100,000 weekly to more than 1,500,000 and its average pagination more than trebled to seventy-two. The *Post* claimed with reason that each issue had at least three readers, which gave it an audience approximating five per cent of the total population weekly. The significance of this audience increase is made more plain by contrasting it with that of *Collier's*, from 300,000 to 521,000 weekly in this same decade, and of *Cosmopolitan*, from 400,000 to 750,000 monthly, which scored its largest gains after its acquisition by William Randolph Hearst in 1905 and a marked increase in the fiction contents of each issue.

The cowboy story did not comprise a significant proportion of the *Post's* fiction offerings until 1907, when it approached 10 per cent of the total. This figure parallels the proportion of cowboy offerings in the other magazines studied over the same span. The most prolific producers of such stories throughout the decade, those whose output makes the largest identifiable bloc, were Emerson Hough, Henry Wallace Phillips, Alfred Henry Lewis, O. Henry, William R. Lighton, Kennett Harris and, towards the end of the decade, Rex Beach.

They distributed their wares widely among the

magazines studied, and their stories all had common major characteristics that stemmed from the earlier writings of Bret Harte and Mark Twain. These included a thoroughly masculine society in a picturesque setting, such as Lewis's "Wolfville" or Hough's "Heart's Desire"; often a continuing central character, such as Phillips's "Red Saunders" or Lighton's "Billy Fortune"; broad and boisterous masculine humor, often verging upon adolescent low comedy; a theatrical plot, or none at all; a tinge of heart-of-gold knight-errantry; explosive action as required, not necessarily with pistols, and exaggerated dialect and mannerisms and costuming designed to distinguish the cowboy from his more combed and curried and timorous fellows.

The contrast afforded by "The Little Eohippus," this story's magazine title, was and remains pronounced. It was the first full-length, cowboy-and-the-lady romance to appear in any of the mass circulation magazines and only the second serial of its type that the *Post* had used. Its predecessor also had been a Rhodesean offering, "The Line of Least Resistance," which appeared in 1910 in four parts and had a melodramatic, Indian-menace, frontier-Gothic climax. For those interested, this writer does not regard two-part stories as proper serials, and notes that *The Virginian* did not appear in serial form but as a series of two-parters and separate short stories that Wister reworked to make the novel, dropping much of the humor in the originals in the process.

The conflict between East and West, heroine and hero, over which Wister agonized in *The Virginian* is absent from this story. As James K. Folsom has noted, "Inherent in the theme of confrontation of one culture with another is the moral valuation of the relative merits of each . . . ." In Rhodes' view, the West was so superior in values, morals, and ethical standards that comparison was impossible and conflict incredible. That this viewpoint can be classed as narrowly provincial, even oppressively parochial, and insufferably chauvinistic is admitted cheerfully. It is offset, perhaps, by Rhodes' Eastern heroine, Ellinor, who had "twenty-seven different kinds of hell in her." After the fashion of women since time began when it came to the man each wanted, she let Jeff Bransford, the Western hero, chase her until she caught him. It is educational to compare Rhodes' handling of her with Wister's "Molly," of whom Wallace Stegner has said, "she had not grown noticeably beyond the mining-camp schoolmarm bequeathed to him [*Wister*] by Bret Harte."

It is advisable also to refute a recent [*1970*] comment by a student of popular culture who said of Rhodes ". . . the *Post* unfortunately convinced him that he needed to insert a love interest and a noble social message into what was otherwise first-rate Western fiction." Rhodesean fiction, by and large, has few women and little love interest, which makes this story one of the exceptions and a major one at that. When Rhodes does come down before the footlights, even as Iago, to proclaim a noble social message, which he did most blatantly in *Stepsons of Light*, it is not because of editorial urgings but despite editorial admonitions.

Rhodes' real message can be clearly seen and keenly felt by those who have the mind and heart to do so. As you read this yarn, consider that Jeff Bransford could have gone Scot-free at his preliminary hearing had he permitted the fair Ellinor to testify in his behalf. Observe that she *wanted* to testify and that he subtly dissuaded her. And why? Because of compromising her virtue! But, you will ask, how could one brief and innocent flirtation, touching in its chaste naiveté, be construed even in New Mexico as compromising a fair maiden's honor? It could not by the canons of today's females; nor, apparently, could it by the standards of the maid involved. It could by Jeff's standards, which were his own, and he played his hand accordingly, risking his neck and thickening the plot thereby.

Note also that the villain in this piece is not villainous because some inexorable System forced him into such a role. He is a twenty-four carat, son-of-a-skunk because he lacks the dignity, decency, and compassion to be otherwise. Observe the forces operating against Jeff. They are not puppets whose strings are pulled by some evil Establishment; they are singularly human human beings, who act and react as they do from very human motives, stimuli, whatever. It is in his hero, in his villain, in his assorted Bearers of the Winchester that Rhodes conveys, as in every other major story he ever wrote, his major message—the West as he had known it and lived it, as it remained forever in his heart, was a West of individuals, not hapless fragments in an oppressed and oppressive agglomerate.

They were individuals who thought little of neck-or-nothing incidents; one throw of the dice; one turn of the cards; "Sydney or the Bush!" Even so did Currier & Ives portray the New Bedford creed, "A dead whale or a stoved boat," which Rhodes found in his own milieu in the tie-fast men, those who tied their catch ropes hard-and-fast to the saddle horn, or to the tree itself, knowing full well that when they caught, whatever was in the loop was theirs or they were its.

That Rhodes idealized the characters he took from life is beyond dispute. For example: the man who in life bore the name Jeff Bransford had a full-blood Oglala mother, a niece of Red Cloud by repute, while his father, William Bransford, was a Virginian who wandered west to become a Mountain Man in the dying days of the beaver trade. When Jeff's riding days were done and his fortunes withered, he spun out his life in El Paso at various lowly tasks but remained a salty *hombre*, labelled plainly "Use No Hooks," until he died.

The story's magazine success was not duplicated when it appeared in book form, more than a year after its *Post* appearance. In common with many an author before and since, and probably forevermore, Rhodes believed firmly that this was due to his publisher's egregious asininity: in this case, the necessity of changing the story's ending for book publication. This involved the last one-third of the story, beginning with Bransford's arrival at *Los Baños de Santa Eulalia del Norte*. There were valid reasons, given the book publishing world at the time, for this insistence upon such a change.

In the magazine version, which has been used here for the first time since 1912, you will note that Jeff goes East to find Ellinor and happiness beside Cayuga's waters. This enabled Rhodes to present his impressions of Easterners as he had known them in this same locale, while pointing up his definite views on the differences between Life's talkers and dreamers and its doers. This was his first fictional attempt to join the discrete halves of his experiential conditioning; the other coming in *Copper Streak Trail* where he became unabashedly Dickensian in depicting the narrow corners of men's lives among "God's Frozen People." Gratifying as this was to Rhodes, and despite the story's magazine success, such an ending did not suit the needs of Henry Holt & Company.

They were publishing a dyed-in-the-saddle-blanket cowboy story, and to have some of its minor characters quoting Hegel and Locke and Berkeley was not within the genre as they knew it. Neither was a cowboy story a "Western" story if it ended amidst a Cornell crew race and a flow of precious repartee. This was due to what had happened to the cowboy story without any assistance, let alone recognition of the change, by the mass circulation magazines. Quite simply, the cowboy story had been taken over by the first of its formula fabulists—Zane Grey, Clarence E. Mulford, William MacLeod Raine, and Charles Alden Seltzer. (Those who may think that the lack of attention to Bertha M. Bower-Sinclair-Cowan is due to careless oversight are advised that it is not.)

Using for springboards such magazines as *Popular*, a "pulp" product of Street & Smith's fiction factory with a circulation of 300,000 twice-a-month, and small circulation, masculine-oriented outdoor magazines, such as *Outing* and *Field and Stream*, the fabulists found reputable publishing houses, such as Harper & Brothers, for book publication to their mutual benefit. By 1912, the year of this story's magazine appearance and that of Grey's *Riders of the Purple Sage* in book form, the latter field belonged to the fabulists. In accordance with the literary equivalent of Gresham's Law, both the rowdy, humorous, picturesque, occasionally raffish cowboy type and Rhodes' Theseus-in-leather-leggings were doomed to lose the sweepstakes of popular demand.

To meet his publisher's wishes, Rhodes altered and mortised his ending to bring the story to its close in New Mexico, where as a "Western" about cowboys it belonged. To him, this was "*an irretrievable loss.*" By retaining his original ending in this edition, it is hoped to show why it can be said of Rhodes that of all those

who have written cowboy stories since Wister made
him and them respectable, he alone was different.

This edition does retain one other difference between magazine and book versions that was necessary
for original book publication. As with most of Rhodes'
longer stories, this one was too short in its magazine
form to compete in the marketplace with the works of
the fabulists. It needed bulk, so to speak, and Rhodes
supplied twenty-six additional pages simply by adding, with very minor changes, a short story about Jeff
Bransford that had appeared in the *Post*, April 24,
1909, as "An Executive Mind." It appears to have
been from its beginning a part of the longer story
Rhodes had in mind, and as the "Prologue" to the
book version, it served to introduce Jeff and delineate
his salient characteristics before he met the woman in
the case. It also gave Rhodes a chance to present his
family's side of how their own homestead in New
Mexico had been usurped, for this aspect of the Prologue was taken directly from life. Rhodes, himself,
is the story's "John Taylor, Junior," while his family
is portrayed accurately, even unto the depiction of his
father being "futile and left-handed all over" when it
came to homesteading. A different facet of the father-
and-son relationship may be found in the characters
of "Old Dad" and "Otey Beach" in Rhodes' later
novel, *The Proud Sheriff*.

One final note may not be amiss in this presently
price-conscious society. When Holt published this

story in 1914 as *Bransford in Arcadia*, it sold for $1.20 net. Given the purchasing power of the dollar then, the present price seems more than reasonable. *¿No es verdad?*

W. H. HUTCHINSON

California State University, Chico
August 31, 1974

CONTENTS

BRANSFORD IN ARCADIA

PROLOGUE

I

THE LONG fall round-up was over. The wagon, home-
ward bound, made camp for the last night out at the
Sinks of Lost River. Most of the men, worn with
threescore nightguards, were buried under their tarps
in the deep sleep of the weary; sound as that of the
just, and much more common.

By the low campfire a few yet lingered: old-timers,
iron men, whose wiry and seasoned strength was toil-
proof—and Leo Ballinger, for whom youth, excitement and unsated novelty served in lieu of fitness.

The "firelighters," working the wide range again
from Ancho to Hueco, from the Mal Pais to Glencoe,
fell silent now, to mark an unstaled miracle.

The clustered lights of Rainbow's End shone redly,

near and low. Beyond, above, dominant, the black, unbroken bulk of Rainbow Range shut out the east. The clear-cut crest mellowed to luminous curves, feathery with far-off pines; the long skyline thrilled with frosty fire, glowed, sparkled—the cricket's chirp was stilled; the slow, late moon rose to a hushed and waiting world.

On the sharp crest she paused, irresolute, tiptoe, quivering, rosily aflush. Above floated a web of gossamer. She leaped up, spurning the black rim; glowed, palpitant, through that filmy lace—and all the desert throbbed with vibrant light.

Cool and sweet and fresh, from maiden leagues of clean, brown earth the desert winds made whisper in grass and fragrant shrub; yucca, mesquite and grease-wood swayed—so softly, you had not known save as the long shadows courtesied and danced.

Leo flung up his hand. The air was wine to him. A year had left the desert still new and strange. "Gee!" he said eloquently.

Headlight nodded. "You're dead right on that point, son. If Christopher K. Columbus had only thought to beach his shallops on the sundown side of this here continent he might have made a name for himself. Just think how much different, hysterically, these United States—"

"*This* United States," corrected Pringle dispassionately. Their fathers had disagreed on the same grammatical point.

Headlight scowled. "By Jings! 'That *this* United

4

Colonies are, and of right ought to be, free and independent States,' " he quoted. "I was goin' to give you something new to exercise your talons on. You sit here every night, ridin' broncs and four-footin' steers, and never grab a horn or waste a loop, not once. Sure things ain't amusin'. Some variety and doubtful accuracy, now, would develop our guessin' gifts."

Aforesaid Smith brandished the end-gate rod. "Them speculations of yours sorter opens up of themselves. If California had been settled first the salmon would now be our national bird instead of the potato. Think of Arizona, mother of Presidents! Seat of government at Milipitas; center of population about Butte; New Jersey howlin' about Nevada trusts!" He impaled a few beef ribs and held them over the glowing embers.

"Georgia and South Carolina would be infested by cow-persons in décolleté leather panties," said Jeff Bransford. "New York and Pennsylvania would be fondly turning a credulous ear to the twenty-fourth consecutive solemn promise of Statehood—with the Senator from Walla Walla urging admission of both as one mighty State with Maryland and Virginia thrown in for luck."

Headlight forgot his pique. "Wouldn't the railroads sound funny, though? Needles and Eastern, Northern Atlantic, Southern Atlantic, Union, Western, Kansas and Central Atlantic! Earnest and continuous demand for a President from east of the Mississippi. All the prize-fights pulled off at Boston."

"Columbus done just right," said Pringle decisively. "You fellers ain't got no imagination a-tall. If this Western country'd been settled first, the maps would read: 'Northeast Territory.—Uninhabitable wilderness; region of storm and snow, roaming savages and fierce wild beasts.' When the intrepid explorer hit the big white weather he'd say, 'Little old San Diego's good enough for me!' Yes, sir!"

"Oh, well, climate alone doesn't account for the charm of this country—nor scenery," said Leo. "You feel it, but you don't know why it is."

"It sure agrees with your by-laws," observed Pringle. "You're a sight changed from the furtive behemoth you was. You'll make a hand yet. But, even now, your dimensions from east to west is plumb fascinatin'. I'd sure admire to have your picture to put in my cornfield."

"Very well, Mr. Pringle: I'll exchange photographs with you," said Leo artlessly. A smothered laugh followed this remark; uncertainty as to what horrible and unnamed use Leo would make of Pringle's pictured face appealed to these speculative minds.

"I've studied out this charm business," said Jeff. "See if I'm not right. It's because there's no habitually old men here to pattern after, to steady us, to make us ashamed of just staying boys. Now and then you hit an octagonal cuss like Wes here, that on a mere count of years and hairs might be sized up as old by the superficial observer. But if I have ever met that man more addicted with vivid nonchalance as to further continuance of educational facilities than this same Also Ran, his number has now escaped me. Really aged old people stay where they was."

"I think, myself, that what makes life so easy and congenial in these latigos and longitudes is the dearth of law and the ladies." Thus Pringle, the cynic.

A fourfold outcry ensued; indignant repudiation of the latter heresy. Their protest rose above the customary subdued and quiet drawl of the out-of-doors man.

"But has the law no defenders?" demanded Leo. "We've got to have laws to make us behave."

"Sure thing! Likewise, 'tis the waves that make the tide come in," said Jeff. "A good law is as handy as a good pocketbook. But law, as simply such, independent of its merits, rouses no enthusiasm in my manly bosom, no more than a signboard the day after Hallowe'en. If it occurs to me in a moment of emotional sanity that the environments of the special case in hand call for a compound fracture of the statutes made and provided—for some totally different cases that happen to be called by the same name—I fall upon it with my glittering hew-gag, without no special wonder. For," he declaimed, "I am endowed by nature with certain inalienable rights, among which are the high justice, the middle, and the low!"

"And who's to be the judge of whether it's a good law or not? You?"

"Me. Me, every time. Some one must. If I let some other man make up my mind I've got to use my judg-

ment—picking the man I follow. By organizing myself into a Permanent Committee of One to do my
own thinking I take my one chance of mistakes instead of two."

"So you believe in doing evil that good may come,
do you?"

"Well," said Jeff judicially, "it seems to be at least
as good a proposition as doing good that evil may
come of it. Why, Capricorn, there isn't one thing we
call wrong, when other men do it, that hasn't been
lawful, some time or other. When to break a law is to
do a wrong, it's evil. When it's doing right to break a
law, it's not evil. Got that? It's not wrong to keep a
just law—and if it's wrong to break an unjust law I
want a new dictionary with pictures of it in the back."

"But laws is useful and excitin' diversions to break
up the monogamy," said Aforesaid. "And it's a dead
easy way to build up a rep. Look at the edge I've got
on you fellows. You're just supposed to be honest—
but I've been proved honest, frequent!"

"Hark!" said Pringle.

A weird sound reached them—the night wrangler,
beguiling his lonely vigil with song.

"Oh, the cuckoo is a pretty bird; she comes in the
    spring————"

"What do you s'pose that night-hawk thinks about
the majesty of the law?" he said. There was a ringing
note in his voice. Smith and Headlight nodded gravely; their lean, brown faces hardened.

8

"You haven't heard of it? Old John Taylor, daddy to yonder warbler, drifted here from the East. Wife and little girl both puny. Taylor takes up a homestead on the Feliz. He wasn't affluent none. I let him have my old paint pony, Freckles—him being knee-sprung and not up to cow-work. To make out an unparalleled team, he got Ed Poe's Billy Bowlegs, née Gambler, him havin' won a new name by a misunderstanding with a prairie-dog hole. Taylor paid Poe for him in work. He was a willin' old rooster, Taylor, but futile and left-handed all over.

"John, Junior, he was only thirteen. Him and the old man moseyed around like two drunk ants, fixin' up a little log house with rock chimbleys, a horse-pen and shelter, rail-fencin' of the little *vegas* to put to crops, and so on.

"Done you good to drop in and hear 'em plan and figger. They was one happy family. How Sis Em'ly bragged about their hens layin'! In the spring we all held a bee and made their *'cequias* for 'em. Baker, he loaned 'em a plow. They dragged big branches over the ground for a harrow. They could milk anybody's cows they was a mind to tame, and the boys took to carryin' over motherless calves for Mis' Taylor to raise. Taylor, he done odd jobs, and they got along real well with their crops. They went into the second winter peart as squirrels.

"But, come spring, Sis wasn't doin' well. They had the Agency doctor. Too high up and too damp, he

said. So the missus and Em'ly they went to Cruces,
where Em'ly could go to school.

"That meant right smart of expense—rentin' a
house and all. So the Johns they hires out. John,
Junior, made his dayboo as wrangler for the Steam
Pitchfork, acquirin' the obvious name of Felix.

"The old man he got a job muckin' in Organ mines.
Kept his hawses in Jeff Isaack's pasture, and Saturday
nights he'd get one and slip down them eighteen miles
to Cruces for Sunday with the folks.

"Well, you know, a homesteader can't be off his
claim more'n six months at a time.

"I reckon if there was ever a homestead taken up in
good faith 'twas the Butterbowl. They knew the land
laws from A to Izzard. Even named their hound pup
Boney Fido!

"But the old man waited at Organ till the last bell
rang, so's to draw down his wages, pay-day. Then he
bundles the folks into his little old wagon and lights
out. Campin' at Casimiro's Well, halfway 'cross, that
ornery Freckles hawse has a fit of malignant nostolgy
and projects off for Butterbowl, afoot, in his hobbles.
Next day, Taylor don't overtake him till the middle of
the evenin', and what with going back and what with
Freckles being hobble-sore, he's two days late in
reachin' home. For Lake, of Agua Chiquite, that prosperous person, had been keeping cases. He entered
contest on the Butterbowl, allegin' abandonment.

"Now, if it was me—but, then, if 'twas me I could
stay away six years and two months without no

10

remonstrances from Lake or his likes. I'm somewhat abandoned myself.

"But poor old Taylor, he's been drug up where they hold biped life unaccountable high. He sits him down resignedly beneath the sky, as the poet says, meek and legal. We all don't abnormally like to precipitate in another man's business, but we makes it up to sorter saunter in on Lake, spontaneous, and evince our disfavor with a rope. But Taylor says, 'No.' He allows the Land Office won't hold him morally responsible for the sinful idiocy of a homesick spotted hawse that's otherwise reliable.

"He's got one more guess comin'. There ain't no sympathies to machinery. Your intentions may be strictly honorable, but if you get your hand caught in the cogs, off it goes, regardless of how handy it is for flankin' calves, holdin' nails, and such things. 'Absent over six months. Entry canceled. Contestant is allowed thirty days' prior right to file. Next.'

"That's the way that decision'll read. It ain't come yet, but it's due soon.

"This here Felix looks at it just like the old man, only different—though he ain't makin' no statements for publication. He come here young, and having acquired the fixed habit of riskin' his neck, regular, for one dollar per each and every diem, shooin' in the reluctant steer, or a fool hawse pirouettin' across the pinnacles with a nosebag on—or, mebbee, just for fun—why, natural, he don't see why life is so sweet or peace so dear as to put up with any damn foolish-

11

ness, as Pat Henry used to say when the boys called on him for a few remarks. He's a some serious-minded boy, that night-hawk, and if signs is any indications, he's fixin' to take an appeal under the Winchester Act. I ain't no seventh son of a son-of-a-gun, but my prognostications are that he presently removes Lake to another and, we trust, a better world."

"Good thing, too," grunted Headlight. "This Lake person is sure-lee a muddy pool."

"Shet your fool head," said Pringle amiably. "You may be on the jury. I'm going to seek my virtuous couch. Glad we don't have to bed no cattle, *viva voce*, this night."

"Ain't he the Latin scholar?" said Headlight admiringly. "They blow about that wire Julius Caesar sent the Associated Press, but old man Pringle done him up for levity and precision when he wrote us the account of his visit to the Denver carnival. Ever hear about it, Sagittarius?"

"No," said Leo. "What did he say?"

"Hic—hock—hike!"

II

ESCONDIDO, half-way of the desert, is designed on simple lines. The railroad hauls water in tank-cars from Dog Cañon. There is one depot, one section-house, and one combination post-office-hotel-store-saloon-stage-station, kept by Ma Sanders and Pappy Sanders, in about the order mentioned. Also, one glorious green cottonwood, one pampered rosebush, jointly the pride and delight of Escondido, ownerless, but cherished by loving care and "toted" tribute of waste water.

Hither came Jeff and Leo, white with the dust of twenty starlit leagues, for accumulated mail of Rainbow South. Horse-feeding, breakfast, gossip with jolly, motherly Ma Sanders, reading and answering of mail—then their beauty nap; so missing the day's event, the passing of the Flyer. When they woke Escondido basked drowsily in the low, westering sun. The far sunset ranges had put off their workaday homespun brown and gray for chameleon hues of purple and amethyst; their deep, cool shadows, edged with trembling rose, reached out across the desert; the velvet air stirred faintly to the promise of the night.

The agent was putting up his switch-lights; from the kitchen came a cheerful clatter of tinware.

"Now we buy some dry goods and wet," said Leo. They went into the store.

"That decision's come!" shrilled Pappy in tremulous excitement. "It's too dum bad! Registered letters from Land Office for Taylor and Lake, besides another for Lake, not registered."

"That one from the Land Office, too?" said Jeff.

"Didn't I jest tell ye? Say, it's a shame! Why don't some of you fellers—— Gosh! If I was only young!"

"It's a travesty on justice!" exclaimed Leo indignantly. "There's really no doubt but that they decided for Lake, I suppose?"

"Not a bit. He's got the law with him. Then him and the Register is old cronies. Guess this other letter is from him unofficial, likely."

Jeff seated himself on a box. "How long has this Lake got to do his filing in, Pappy?"

"Thirty days from the time he signs the receipt for this letter—dum him!"

"Some one ought to kidnap him," said Leo.

"Why, that's illegal!" Jeff nursed his knee, turned his head to one side and chanted thoughtfully:

> "Said the little Eohippus,
>   'I'm going to be a horse,
> And on my middle finger-nails
>   To run my earthly course'————"

He broke off and smiled at Leo indulgently. Leo glanced at him sharply; this was Jeff's warsong aforetime. But it was to Pappy that Jeff spoke:

"Dad, you're a better'n any surgeon. Wish you'd go out and look at Leo's horse. His ankle's all swelled up. I'll be mixin' me up a toddy, if Ma's got any hot water. I'm feeling kinder squeamish."

"Hot toddy, this weather? Some folks has queer tastes," grumbled Pappy. "Ex-*cuse* me! Me and Leo'll go look at the Charley-horse. That bottle under the shelf is the best." He bustled out. But Jeff caught Ballinger by the sleeve.

14

"Will you hold my garments while I stone Stephen?" he hissed.

"I will," said Leo, meeting Jeff's eye. "Hit him once for me."

"Move the lever to the right, you old retrograde, and get Pappy to gyratin' on his axis some fifteen or twenty minutes, you listenin' reverently. Meanwhile, I'll make the necessary incantations. Git! Don't look so blamed intelligent, or Pappy'll be suspicious."

Bransford hastened to the kitchen. "Ma Sanders, a bronc fell on me yesterday and my poor body is one big stone bruise. Can I borrow some boiling water to mix a small prescription, or maybe seven? One when you first feel like it, and repeat at intervals, the doctor says."

"Don't you get full in *my* house, Jeff Bransford, or I'll feed you to the hawgs. You take three doses, and that'll be a-plenty for you."

Jeff put the steaming kettle on the rusty store stove, used as a waste-paper basket through the long summer. Touching off the papers with a match, he smashed an empty box and put it in. Then he went into the post-office corner and laid impious hands on the United States Mail.

First he steamed open Lake's unregistered letter from the Land Office. It was merely a few typewritten lines, having no reference to the Butterbowl: "Enclosing the Plat of TP. 14 E. of First Guide Meridan East Range S. of 3d Standard Parallel South, as per request."

He paused to consider. His roving eye lit on the wall, where the Annual Report of the Governor of New Mexico hung from a nail. "The very thing," he said. Pasted in the report was a folded map of the Territory. This he cut out, refolded it till it slipped in the violated envelope, dabbed the flap neatly with Pappy's mucilage, and returned the letter to its proper pigeonhole.

He replenished the fire with another box, subjected Lake's registered letter to the steaming process and opened it with delicate caution. It was the decision; it was in Lake's favor; and it went into the fire. Substituting for it the Plat of TP. 14 and the accompanying letter he resealed it with workmanlike neatness, and then restored it with a final inspection. "The editor sits on the madhouse floor, and pla-ays with the straws in his hair!" he murmured, beaming with complacent pride and reaching for the bottle.

Pappy and Leo found him with his hands to the blaze, shivering. "I feel like I was going to have a chill," he complained. But with a few remedial measures he recuperated sufficiently to set off for Rainbow after supper.

"Charley's ankle seems better," said Leo artlessly.

"Don't you lay no stress on Charley's ankle," said Jeff, in a burst of confidence. "Where ignorance is bliss, 'tis folly to be otherwise. Just let Charley's ankle slip your memory."

The following day Bransford drew rein at Wes Pringle's shack and summoned him forth.

16

"Mr. John Wesley Also Ran Pringle," he said impressively, "I have taken a horse-ride over here to put you through your cataclysm. Will you truthfully answer the rebuses I shall now propound to the best of your ability, and govern yourself accordingly till the surface of Hades congeals to glistening bergs, and that with no unseemly curiosity?"

"Is it serious?" asked Pringle anxiously.

"This is straight talk."

Pringle took a long look and held up his hand. "I will," he said soberly.

"John Wesley, do you or do you not believe Stephen W. Lake, of Agua Chiquite, to be a low-down, coniferous skunk by birth, inclination and training?"

"I do."

"John Wesley, do you or do you not possess the full confidence and affection of Felix, the night-hawk, otherwise known and designated as John Taylor, Junior, of Butterbowl, Esquire?"

"I do."

"Do you, John Wesley Pringle, esteem me, Jeff Bransford, irrespective of color, sex or previous condition of turpitude, to be such a one as may be safely tied to when all the hitching-posts is done pulled up, and will you now promise to love, honor and obey me till the cows come home, or till further orders?"

"I do—I will. And may God have mercy on my soul."

"Here are your powders, then. Do you go and locate the above-mentioned and described Felix, and impart to him, under the strict seal of secrecy, these tidings, to wit, namely: That you have a presentiment, almost amounting to conviction, that the Butterbowl contest is decided in Lake's favor, but that your further presentiments is that said Lake will not use his prior right. If Taylor should get such a decision from the Land Office don't let him or Felix say a word to no one. If Mr. B. Body should ask, tell 'em 'twas a map, or land laws, or something. Moreover, said Felix he is not to stab, cut, pierce or otherwise mutilate said Lake, nor to wickedly, maliciously, feloniously and unlawfully fire at or upon the person of said Lake with any rifle, pistol, musket or gun, the same being then and there loaded with powder and with balls, shots, bullets or slugs of lead or other metal. You see to that, personal. I'd go to him myself, but he don't know me well enough to have confidence in my divinations.

"You promulgate these prophecies as your sole personal device and construction—*sabe?* Then, thirty days after Lake signs a receipt for his decision—and you will take steps to inform yourself of that—you sidle casually down to Roswell with old man Taylor and see that he puts preëmption papers on the Butterbowl. Selah!"

III

THE first knowledge Lake had of the state of affairs was when the Steam Pitchfork punchers informally extended to him the right hand of fellowship (hitherto withheld) under the impression that he had generously abstained from pushing home his vantage. When, in the midflood of his unaccountable popularity, the situation dawned upon him, he wisely held his peace. He was a victim of the accomplished fact. Taylor had already filed his preëmption. So Lake reaped volunteer harvest of good-will, bearing his honors in graceful silence.

On Lake's next trip to Escondido, Pappy Sanders laid aside his marked official hauteur. Lake stayed several days, praised the rosebush and Ma Sanders' cookery, and indulged in much leisurely converse with Pappy. Thereafter he had a private conference with Stratton, the Register of the Roswell Land Office. His suspicion fell quite naturally on Felix, and on Jeff as accessory during the fact.

So it was that, when Jeff and Leo took in Roswell fair (where Jeff won a near-prize at the roping match), Hobart, the United States Marshal, came to their room. After introducing himself he said:

"Mr. Stratton would like to see you, Mr. Bransford."

"Why, that's all right!" said Jeff genially. "Some of my very great grandfolks was Dacotahs and I've got my name in 'Who's Sioux'—but I'm not proud! Trot him around. Exactly who is Stratton, anyhow?"

"He's the Register of the Land Office—and he wants to see you there on very particular business. I'd go if I was you," said the Marshal significantly.

"Oh, that way!" said Jeff. "Is this an arrest, or do you just give me this *in*-vite semi-officiously?"

"You accuse yourself, sir. Were you expecting arrest? That sounds like a bad conscience."

"Don't you worry about my conscience. 'If I've ever done anything I'm sorry for I'm glad of it.' Now this Stratton party—is he some aged and venerable? 'Cause, if he is, I waive ceremony and seek him in his lair at the witching hour of two this *tarde*. And if not, not."

"He's old enough—even if there were no other reasons."

"Never mind any other reasons. It shall never be said that I fail to reverence gray hairs. I'll be there."

"I guess I'll just wait and see that you go," said the Marshal.

"Have you got any papers for me?" asked Jeff politely.

"No."

"This is my room," said Jeff. "This is my fist. This is me. That is my door. Open it, Leo. Mr. Hobart, you will now make rapid forward motions with your feet, alternately, like a man removing his company from where it is not desired—or I'll go through you like a domesticated cyclone. See you at two, sharp!" Hobart obeyed. He was a good judge of men.

Jeff closed the door. " 'We went upon the battle-field,' " he said plaintively, " 'before us and behind us, and every which-a-way we looked, we seen a roscer-hinus.' We went into another field—behind us and

20

before us, and every which-a-way we looked, we seen a rhinusorus. Mr. Lake has been evidently browsin' and pe-rusing around, and poor old Pappy, not being posted, has likely been narratin' about Charley's ankle and how I had a chill. Wough-ough!"

"It looks that way," confessed Leo. "*Did* you have a chill, Jeff?"

Jeff's eyes crinkled. "Not so nigh as I am now. But shucks! I've been in worse emergencies, and I always emerged. Thanks be, I can always do my best when I have to. Oh, what a tangled web we weave when we don't keep in practice! If I'd just come out straight-forward and declared myself to Pappy, he'd 'a' tightened up his drawstrings and forgot all about my chill. But, no, well as I know from long experience that good old human nature's only too willin' to do the right thing and the fair thing—if somebody'll only tip it off to 'em—I must play a lone hand and not even call for my partner's best. Well, I'm goin' to ramify around and scrutinize this here Stratton's numbers, equipments and disposition. Meet me in the office at the fatal hour!"

The Marshal wore a mocking smile. Stratton, large, florid, well-fed and eminently respectable, turned in his revolving chair with a severe and majestic motion; adjusted his glasses in a prolonged and offensive examination, and frowned portentously.

"Fine large day, isn't it?" observed Jeff affably. "Beautiful little city you have here." He sank into a chair. Smile and attitude were of pleased and sprightly anticipation.

A faint flush showed beneath Stratton's neatly-trimmed mutton-chops. Such jaunty bearing was exasperating to offended virtue. "Ah—who is this other person, Mr. Hobart?"

"Pardon my rudeness!" Jeff sprang up and bowed brisk apology. "Mr. Stratton, allow me to present Mr. Ballinger, a worthy representative of the Yellow Press. Mr. Stratton—Mr. Ballinger!"

"I have a communication to make to you," said the displeased Mr. Stratton, in icy tones, "which, in your own interest, should be extremely private." The Marshal whispered to him; Stratton gave Leo a fiercely intimidating glare.

"Communicate away," said Jeff airily. "Excommunicate, if you want to. Mr. Ballinger, as a citizen, is part owner of this office. If you want to bar him you'll have to change the venue to your private residence. And then I won't come."

"Very well, sir!" Mr. Stratton rose, inflated his chest and threw back his head. His voice took on a steady roll. "Mr. Bransford, you stand under grave displeasure of the law! You are grievously suspected of being cognizant of, if not actually accessory to, the robbery of the United States Mail by John Taylor, Junior, at Escondido, on the eighteenth day of last October. You may not be aware of it, but you have an excellent chance of serving a term in the penitentiary!"

22

Jeff pressed his hands between his knees and leaned forward. "I'm sure I'd never be satisfied there," he said, with conviction. His white teeth flashed in an ingratiatory smile. "But why suspect young John?—why not old John?" He paused, looking at the Register attentively. "H'm!—you're from Indiana, I believe, Mr. Stratton?" he said.

"The elder Taylor, on the day in question, is fully accounted for," said Hobart. "Young Taylor claims to have passed the night at Willow Springs, alone. But no one saw him from breakfast time the seventeenth till noon on the nineteenth."

"He rarely ever has any one with him when he's alone. That may account for them not seeing him at Willow," suggested Jeff. He did not look at Hobart, but regarded Stratton with an air of deep meditation.

The Register paced the floor slowly, ponderously, with an impressive pause at each turn, tapping his left hand with his eyeglass to score his points. "He had ample time to go to Escondido and return. The envelope in which Mr. Lake's copy of this office's decision in the Lake-Taylor contest was enclosed has been examined. It bears unmistakable signs of having been tampered with." Turning to mark the effect of these tactics, he became aware of his victim's contemplative gaze. It disconcerted him. He resumed his pacing. Jeff followed him with a steady eye.

"In the same mail I sent Mr. Lake another letter. The envelope was unfortunately destroyed, Mr. Lake suspecting nothing. A map had been substituted for its contents, and they, in turn, were substituted for the decision in the registered letter, with the evident intention of depriving Mr. Lake of his prior right to file."

"By George! It sounds probable." Jeff laughed derisively. "So that's it! And here we all thought Lake let it go out of giddy generosity! My stars, but won't he get the horse-smile when the boys find out?"

Stratton controlled himself with an effort. "We have decided not to push the case against you if you will tell what you know," he began.

Jeff lifted his brows. "*We?* And who's *we?* You two? I should have thought this was a postoffice lay."

"We are investigating the affair," explained Hobart.

"I see! As private individuals. Yes, yes. Does Lake pay you by the day or by the job?"

Stratton, blazing with anger, smote his palm heavily with his fist. "Young man! Young man! Your insolence is unbearable! We are trying to spare you—as you had no direct interest in the matter and doubtless concealed your guilty knowledge through a mistaken and distorted sense of honor. But you tempt us—you tempt us! You don't seem to realize the precarious situation in which you stand."

"What I don't see," said Jeff, in puzzled tones, "is why you bother to spare me at all. If you can prove this, why don't you cinch me and Felix both? Why do you want me to tell you what you already know? And if you can't prove it—who the hell cares what you suspect?"

"We will arrest you," said Stratton thickly, "just as soon as we can make out the papers!"

"Turn your wolf loose, you four-flushers! You may make me trouble, but you can't prove anything. Speaking of trouble—how about you, Mr. Stratton?" As a spring leaps, released from highest tension, face and body and voice flashed from passive indolence to sudden, startling attack. His arm lashed swiftly out as if to deliver the swordsman's stabbing thurst; the poised body followed up to push the stroke home. "You think your secret safe, don't you? It's been some time ago."

Words only—yet it might have been a very sword's point past Stratton's guard. For the Register flinched, staggered, his arrogant face grew mottled, his arm went up. He fell back a step, silent, quivering, leaning heavily on a chair. The Marshal gave him a questioning glance. Jeff kept on.

"You're prominent in politics, business, society, the church. You've a family to think of. It's up to you, Mr. Stratton. Is it worth while? Had we better drop it with a dull, sickening thud?"

Stratton collapsed into the chair, a shapeless bundle, turning a shriveled, feeble face to the Marshal in voiceless imploring.

Unhesitating, Hobart put a hand on his shoulder. "That's all right, old man! We won't give you away. Brace up!" He nodded Jeff to the door. "You win!" he said. Leo followed on tiptoe.

"Why, the poor old duck!" said Jeff remorsefully,

in the passage. "Wish I hadn't come down on him so hard. I overdid it that time. Still, if I hadn't——"

At the Hondo Bridge Jeff looked back and waved a hand. "Good-by, old town! Now we go, gallopy-trot, gallopy, gallopy-trot!" He sang, and the ringing hoofs kept time and tune,

"Florence Mehitabel Genevieve Jane,
She came home in the wind an' the rain,
She came home in the rain an' the snow;
'Ain't a-goin' to leave my home any mo'!' "

"Jeff," said the mystified Ballinger, spurring up beside him, "what has the gray-haired Register done? Has murder stained his hands with gore?"

Jeff raised his bridle hand.

"Gee! Leo, I don't know! I just taken a chance!

CHAPTER I

THE PITCHER THAT WENT TO
THE WELL

"When I bend my head low and listen at the ground,
I can hear vague voices that I used to know,
Stirring in dim places, faint and restless sound;
I remember how it was when the grass began to grow."
                    —*Song of The Wandering Dust,*
                              Anna Hempstead Branch

THE PINES thinned as she neared Rainbow Rim, the
turfy glades grew wider; she had glimpses of open
country beyond—until, at last, crossing a little spit
of high ground, she came to the fairest spot in all her
voyage of exploration and discovery. She sank down
on a fallen log with a little sigh of delight.

The steep bank of a little cañon broke away at her
feet—a cañon which here marked the frontier of the
pines, its farther side overgrown with mahogany bush
and chaparral—a cañon that fell in long, sinuous

27

curves from the silent mystery of forest on Rainbow Crest behind her, to widen just below into a rolling land, parked with green-black powderpuffs of juniper and cedar; and so passed on to mystery again, twisting away through the folds of the low and bare gray hills to the westward, ere the last stupendous plunge over the Rim to the low desert, a mile toward the level of the waiting sea.

Facing the explorer, across the little cañon, a clear spring bubbled from the hillside and fell with pleasant murmur and tinkle to a pool below, fringed with lush emerald—a spring massed about with wild grapevine, shining reeds of arrow-weed; a tangle of grateful greenery, jostling eagerly for the life-giving water. Draped in clinging vines, slim acacias struggled up through the jungle; the exquisite fragrance of their purple bells gave a final charm to the fairy chasm.

But the larger vision! The nearer elfin beauty dwindled, was lost, forgotten. Afar, through a narrow cleft in the gray westward hills, the explorer's eye leaped out over a bottomless gulf to a glimpse of shining leagues midway of the desert greatness—an ever-widening triangle that rose against the peaceful west to long foothill reaches, to a misty mountain parapet, far-beckoning, whispering of secrets, things dreamed of, unseen, beyond the framed and slender arc of vision. A land of enchantment and mystery, decked with strong barbaric colors, blue and red and yellow, brown and green and gray; whose changing ebb and flow, by some potent sorcery of atmosphere, distance and angle, altered, daily, hourly; deepening, fading, combining into new and fantastic lines and shapes, to melt again as swiftly to others yet more bewildering.

The explorer? It may be mentioned in passing that any other would have found that fairest prospect even more wonderful than did the explorer, Miss Ellinor Hoffman. We will attempt no clear description of Miss Ellinor Hoffman. Dusky-beautiful she was; crisp, fresh and sparkling; tall, vigorous, active, strong. Yet she was more than merely beautiful—warm and frank and young; brave and kind and true. Perhaps, even more than soft curves, lips, glory of hair or bewildering eyes, or all together, her chiefest charm was her manner, her frank friendliness. Earth was sweet to her, sweeter for her.

This by way of aside and all to no manner of good. You have no picture of her in your mind. Remember only that she was young—

"The stars to drink from and the sky to dance on"

—young and happy, and therefore beautiful; that the sun was shining in a cloudless sky, the south wind sweet and fresh, buds in the willow.

.   .   .   .

The peace was rent and shivered by strange sounds, as of a giant falling downstairs. There was a crash of breaking boughs beyond the cañon, a glint of color, a swift black body hurtling madly through the shrub-

29

bery. The girl shrank back. There was no time for thought, hardly for alarm. On the farther verge the bushes parted; an apparition hurled arching through the sunshine, down the sheer hill—a glorious and acrobatic horse, his black head low between his flashing feet; red nostrils wide with rage and fear; foam flecks white on the black shoulders; a tossing mane; a rider, straight and tall, superb—to all seeming an integral part of the horse, pitch he never so wildly.

The girl held her breath through the splintered seconds. She thrilled at the shock and storm of them, straining muscles and white hoofs, lurching, stumbling, sliding, lunging, careening in perilous arcs. She saw stones that rolled with them or bounded after; a sombrero whirled above the dust and tumult like a dilatory parachute; a six-shooter jolted up into the air. Through the dust clouds there were glimpses of a watchful face, hair blown back above it; a broken rein snapped beside it, saddle-strings streamed out behind; a supple body that swung from curve to easy curve against shock and plunge, that swayed and poised and clung, and held its desperate dominion still. The saddle slipped forward; with a motion incredibly swift, as a hat is whipped off in a gust of wind, it whisked over withers and neck and was under the furious feet. Swifter, the rider! Cat-quick, he swerved, lit on his feet, leaped aside.

Alas, oh, rider beyond compare, undefeated champion, Pride of Rainbow! Alas, that such thing should be recorded! He leaped aside to shun the black frantic

30

death at his shoulder; his feet were in the treacherous vines: he toppled, grasped vainly at an acacia, catapulted out and down, head first; so lit, crumpled and fell with a prodigious splash into the waters of the pool! *Ay di mi, Alhama!*

The blankets lay strewn along the hill; but observe that the long lead rope of the hackamore (a "hackamore," properly *jaquima*, is, for your better understanding, merely a rope halter) was coiled at the saddle-horn, held there by a stout hornstring. As the black reached the level the saddle was at his heels. To kick was obvious, to go away not less so; but this new terror clung to the maddened creature in his frenzied flight—between his legs, in the air, at his heels, his hip, his neck. A low tree leaned from the hillside; the aërial saddle caught in the forks of it, the bronco's head was jerked round, he was pulled to his haunches, overthrown; but the tough hornstring broke, the freed coil snapped out at him; he scrambled up and bunched his glorious muscles in a vain and furious effort to outrun the rope that dragged at his heels, and so passed from sight beyond the next curve.

Waist-deep in the pool sat the hatless horseman, or perhaps horseless horseman were the juster term, steeped in a profound calm. That last phrase has a familiar sound; Mark Twain's, doubtless—but, all things considered, steeped is decidedly the word. One gloved hand was in the water, the other in the muddy margin of the pool: he watched the final evolution of his late mount with meditative interest. The saddle

31

was freed at last, but its ex-occupant still sat there, lost in thought. Blood trickled, unnoted, down his forehead.

The last stone followed him into the pool; the echoes died on the hills. The spring resumed its pleasant murmur, but the tinkle of its fall was broken by the mimic waves of the pool. Save for this troubled sloshing against the banks, the slow-settling dust and the contemplative bust of the one-time centaur, no trace was left to mark the late disastrous invasion.

The invader's dreamy and speculative gaze followed the dust of the trailing rope. He opened his lips twice or thrice, and spoke, after several futile attempts, in a voice mild, but clearly earnest:

"Oh, you little eohippus!"

The spellbound girl rose. Her hand was at her throat; her eyes were big and round, and her astonished lips were drawn to a round, red O.

Sharp ears heard the rustle of her skirts, her soft gasp of amazement. The merman turned his head briskly, his eye met hers. One gloved hand brushed his brow; a broad streak of mud appeared there, over which the blood meandered uncertainly. He looked up at the maid in silence: in silence the maid looked down at him. He nodded, with a pleasant smile.

"Good-morning!" he said casually.

At this cheerful greeting, the astounded maid was near to tumbling after, like Jill of the song.

"Er—good-morning!" she gasped.

Silence. The merman reclined gently against the bank with a comfortable air of satisfaction. The color came flooding back to her startled face.

"Oh, are you hurt?" she cried.

A puzzled frown struggled through the mud.

"Hurt?" he echoed. "Who, me? . . . Why, no—leastwise, I guess not."

He wiggled his fingers, raised his arms, wagged his head doubtfully and slowly, first sidewise and then up and down; shook himself guardedly, and finally raised tentative boot-tips to the surface. After this painstaking inspection he settled contentedly back again.

"Oh, no, I'm all right," he reported. "Only I lost a big, black, fine, young, nice horse somehow. You ain't seen nothing of him, have you?"

"Then why don't you get out?" she demanded. "I believe you are hurt."

"Get out? Why, yes, ma'am. Certainly. Why not?" But the girl was already beginning to clamber down, grasping the shrubbery to aid in the descent.

Now the bank was steep and sheer. So the merman rose, tactfully clutching the grapevines behind him as a plausible excuse for turning his back. It followed as a corollary of this generous act that he must needs be lame, which he accordingly became. As this mishap became acute, his quick eyes roved down the cañon, where he saw what gave him pause; and he groaned sincerely under his breath. For the black horse had taken to the parked uplands, the dragging rope had tangled in a snaggy tree-root, and he was tracing weary circles in bootless effort to be free.

Tactful still, the dripping merman hobbled to the nearest shade wherefrom the luckless black horse should be invisible, eclipsed by the intervening ridge, and there sank down in a state of exhaustion, his back to a friendly tree-trunk.

CHAPTER II

FIRST AID

"Oh woman! in our hours of ease
Uncertain, coy and hard to please;
But seen too oft, familiar with thy face
We first endure, then pity, then embrace!"

A MOMENT later the girl was beside him, pity in her eyes.

"Let me see that cut on your head," she said. She dropped on her knee and parted the hair with a gentle touch.

"Why, you're real!" breathed the injured near-centaur, beaming with wonder and gratification.

She sat down limply and gave way to wild laughter.

"So are you!" she retorted. "Why, that is exactly what I was thinking! I thought maybe I was asleep and having an extraordinary dream. That wound on your head is not serious, if that's all." She brushed back a wisp of hair that blew across her eyes.

"I hurt this head just the other day," observed the bedraggled victim, as one who has an assortment of heads from which to choose. He pulled off his soaked gloves and regarded them ruefully. " 'Them that go down to deep waters!' That was a regular triumph of matter over mind, wasn't it?"

"It's a wonder you're alive! My! How frightened I was! Aren't you hurt—truly? Ribs or anything?"

The patient's elbows made a convulsive movement to guard the threatened ribs.

"Oh, no, ma'am. I ain't hurt a bit—indeed I ain't," he said truthfully; but his eyes had the languid droop of one who says the thing that is not. "Don't you worry none about me—not one bit. Sorry I frightened you. That black horse now——" He stopped to consider fully the case of the black horse. "Well, you see, ma'am, that black horse, he ain't exactly right plumb gentle." His eyelids drooped again.

The girl considered. She believed him—both that he was not badly hurt and that the black horse was not exactly gentle. And her suspicions were aroused. His slow drawl was getting slower; his cowboyese broader —a mode of speech quite inconsistent with that first sprightly remark about the little eohippus. What manner of cowboy was this, from whose tongue a learned scientific term tripped spontaneously in so stressful a moment—who quoted scraps of the litany unaware? Also, her own eyes were none of the slowest.

36

She had noted that the limping did not begin until he was clear of the pool. Still, that might happen if one were excited; but this one had been singularly calm, "more than usual ca'm," she mentally quoted. . . . Of course, if he really were badly hurt—which she didn't believe one bit—a little bruised and jarred, maybe— the only thing for her to do would be to go back to camp and get help. . . . That meant the renewal of Lake's hateful attentions and—for the other girls, the sharing of her find. . . . She stole another look at her find and thrilled with all the pride of the discoverer. . . . No doubt he was shaken and bruised, after all. He must be suffering. What a splendid rider he was!

"What made you so absurd? Why didn't you get out of the water, then, if you are not hurt?" she snapped suddenly.

The drooped lids raised; brown eyes looked steadily into brown eyes.

"I didn't want to wake up," he said.

The candor of this explanation threw her, for the moment, into a vivid and becoming confusion. The dusky roses leaped to her cheeks; the long, dark lashes quivered and fell. Then she rose to the occasion.

"And how about the little eohippus?" she demanded. "That doesn't seem to go well with some of your other talk."

"Oh!" He regarded her with pained but unflinching innocence. "The Latin, you mean? Why, ma'am, that's most all the Latin I know—that and some more

37

big words in that song. I learned that song off of Frank John, just like a poll-parrot."

"Sing it! And eohippus isn't Latin. It's Greek."

"Why, ma'am, I can't, just now—I'm so muddy; but I'll tell it to you. Maybe I'll sing it to you some other time." A sidelong glance accompanied this little suggestion. The girl's face was blank and non-committal; so he resumed: "It goes like this:

> "Said the little Eohippus,
>   'I'm going to be a horse,
> And on my middle finger-nails
>   To run my earthly course'————

No; that wasn't the first. It begins:

> "There was once a little animal
>   No bigger than a fox,
> And on five toes he scampered————

"Of course you know, ma'am—Frank John he told me about it—that horses were little like that, 'way back. And this one he set his silly head that he was going to be a really-truly horse, like the song says. And folks told him he couldn't—couldn't possibly be done, nohow. And sure enough he did. It's a foolish song, really. I only sing parts of it when I feel like that—like it couldn't be done and I was going to do it, you know. The boys call it my song. Look here, ma'am!" He fished in his vest pocket and produced tobacco and papers, matches—last of all, a tiny turquoise horse, an inch long. "I had a jeweler-man put

38

five toes on his feet once to make him be a little eohippus. Going to make a watch charm of him sometime. He's a lucky little eohippus, I think. Peso gave him to me when—never mind when. Peso's a Mescalero Indian, you know, chief of police at the agency." He gingerly dropped the little horse into her eager palm.

It was a singularly grotesque and angular little beast, high-stepping, high-headed, with a level stare, at once complacent and haughty. Despite the first unprepossessing rigidity of outline, there was somehow a sprightly air, something endearing, in the stiff, purposed stride, the alert, inquiring ears, the stern and watchful eye. Each tiny hoof was faintly graven to semblance of five tinier toes; there, the work showed fresh.

"The cunning little monster!" Prison grime was on him; she groomed and polished at his dingy sides until the wonderful color shone out triumphant. "What is it that makes him such a dear? Oh, I know. It's something—well, childlike, you know. Think of the grown-up child that toiled with pride and joy at the making of him—dear me, how many lifetimes since!—and fondly put him by as a complete horse." She held him up in the sun: the ingrate met her caress with the same obdurate and indomitable glare. She laughed her rapturous delight: "There! How much better you look! Oh, you darling! Aren't you absurd? Straight-backed, stiff-legged, thick-necked, square-headed—and that ridiculously baleful eye! It's too high up and too far

39

forward, you know—and your ears are too big—and you have such a malignant look! Never mind; now that you're all nice and clean, I'm going to reward you." Her lips just brushed him—the lucky little eohippus.

The owner of the lucky little horse was not able to repress one swift, dismal glance at his own vast dishevelment, nor, as his shrinking hands, entirely of their own volition, crept stealthily to hiding, the slightest upward rolling of a hopeful eye toward the leaping waters of the spring; but, if one might judge from her sedate and matter-of-fact tones, that eloquent glance was wasted on the girl.

"You ought to take better care of him, you know," she said as she restored the little monster to his owner. Then she laughed. "Hasn't he a fierce and warlike appearance, though?"

"Sure. That's resolution. Look at those legs!" said the owner fondly. "He spurns the ground. He's going somewheres. He's going to be a horse! And them ears —one cocked forward and the other back, strictly on the *cuidado*! He'll make it. He'll certainly do to take along! Yes, ma'am, I'll take right good care of him." He regarded the homely beast with awe; he swathed him in cigarette papers with tenderest care. "I'll leave him at home after this. He might get hurt. I might sometime want to give him to—somebody."

The girl sprang up.

"Now I must get some water and wash that head," she announced briskly.

"Oh, no—I can't let you do that. I can walk. I ain't hurt a bit, I keep telling you." In proof of which he walked to the pool with a palpably clever assumption of steadiness. The girl fluttered solicitous at his elbow. Then she ran ahead, climbed up to the spring and extended a firm, cool hand, which he took shamelessly, and so came to the fairy waterfall.

Here he made himself presentable as to face and hands. It is just possible there was a certain expectancy in his eye as he neared the close of these labors; but if there were it passed unnoted. The girl bathed the injured head with her handkerchief, and brushed back his hair with a dainty caressing motion that thrilled him until the color rose beneath the tan. There was a glint of gray in the wavy black hair, she noted.

She stepped back to regard her handiwork. "Now you look better!" she said approvingly. Then, slightly flurried, not without a memory of a previous and not dissimilar remark of hers, she was off up the hill: whence, despite his shocked protest, she brought back the lost gun and hat.

Her eyes were sparkling when she returned, her face glowing. Ignoring his reproachful gaze, she wrung out her handkerchief, led the patient firmly down the hill and to his saddle, made him trim off a saddle-string, and bound the handkerchief to the wound. She fitted the sombrero gently.

"There! Don't this head feel better now?" she queried gayly, with fine disregard for grammar. "And now what? Won't you come back to camp with me?

41

Mr. Lake will be glad to put you up or to let you have a horse. Do you live far away? I do hope you are not one of those Rosebud men. Mr. La——" She bit her speech off midword.

"No men there except this Mr. Lake?" asked the cowboy idly.

"Oh, yes; there's Mr. Herbert—he's gone riding with Lettie—and Mr. White; but it was Mr. Lake who got up the camping party. Mother and Aunt Lot, and a crowd of us girls—La Luz girls, you know. Mother and I are visiting Mr. Lake's sister. He's going to give us a masquerade ball when we get back, next week."

The cowboy looked down his nose for consultation, and his nose gave a meditative little tweak.

"What Lake is it? There's some several Lakes round here. Is it Lake of Aqua Chiquite—wears his hair décolleté; talks like he had a washboard in his throat; tailor-made face; walks like a duck on stilts; general sort of pouter-pigeon effect?"

At this envenomed description, Miss Ellinor Hoffman promptly choked.

"I don't know anything about your Aqua Chiquite. I never heard of the place before. He is a banker in Arcadia. He keeps a general store there. You must know him, surely." So far her voice was rather stern and purposely resentful, as became Mr. Lake's guest; but there were complications, rankling memories of Mr. Lake—of unwelcome attentions persistently forced upon her. She spoiled the rebuke by adding

42

tartly, "But I think he is the man you mean!" and felt her wrongs avenged.

The cowboy's face cleared.

"Well, I don't use Arcadia much, you see. I mostly range down Rainbow River. Arcadia folks—why, they're mostly newcomers, health-seekers and people just living on their incomes—not working folks much, except the railroaders and lumbermen. Now about getting home. You see, ma'am, some of the boys are riding down that way"—he jerked his thumb to indicate the last flight of the imperfectly gentle horse— "and they're right apt to see my runaway eohippus and sure to see the rope-drag; so they'll likely amble along the back track to see how much who's hurt. So I guess I'd better stay here. They may be along most any time. Thank you kindly, just the same. Of course, if they don't come at all——Is your camp far?"

"Not—not very," said Ellinor. The mere fact was that Miss Ellinor had set out ostensibly for a sketching expedition with another girl, had turned aside to explore, and exploring had fetched a circuit that had left her much closer to her starting-place than to her goal. He misinterpreted the slight hesitation.

"Well, ma'am, thank you again; but I mustn't be keeping you longer. I really ought to see you safe back to your camp; but—you'll understand—under the circumstances—you'll excuse me?"

He did not want to implicate Mr. Lake, so he took a limping step forward to justify his rudeness.

"And you hardly able to walk? Ridiculous! What I

ought to do is to go back to camp and get some one—get Mr. White to help you." Thus, at once accepting his unspoken explanation, and offering her own apology in turn, she threw aside the air of guarded hostility that had marked the last minutes and threw herself anew into this joyous adventure. "When—or if—your friends find you, won't it hurt you to ride?" she asked, and smiled deliberate encouragement.

"I can be as modest as anybody when there's anything to be modest about; but in this case I guess I'll now declare that I can ride anything that a saddle will stay on. . . . I reckon," he added reflectively, "the boys'll have right smart to say about me being throwed."

"But you weren't thrown! You rode magnificently!" Her eyes flashed admiration.

"Yes'm. That's what I hoped you'd say," said the admired one complacently. "Go on, ma'am. Say it again."

"It was splendid! The saddle turned—that's all!"

He slowly surveyed the scene of his late exploit.

"Ye—es, that was some riding—for a while," he admitted. "But you see, that saddle now, scarred up that way—why, they'll think the eohippus wasted me and then dragged the saddle off under a tree. Least-ways, they'll say they think so, frequent. Best not to let on and to make no excuses. It'll be easier that way. We're great on guying here. That's most all the fun we have. We sure got this joshing game down fine. Just wondering what all the boys'd say—that was why I

44

didn't get out of the water at first, before—before I thought I was asleep, you know."

"So you'll actually tell a lie to keep from being thought a liar? I'm disappointed in you."

"Why, ma'am, I won't say anything. They'll do the talking."

"It'll be deceitful, just the same," she began, and checked herself suddenly. A small twinge struck her at the thought of poor Maud, really sketching on Thumb Butte, and now disconsolately wondering what had become of lunch and fellow-artist; but she quelled this pang with a sage thought of the greatest good to the greatest number, and clapped her hands in delight. "Oh, what a silly I am, to be sure! I've got a lunch basket up there, but I forgot all about it in the excitement. I'm sure there's plenty for two. Shall I bring it down to you or can you climb up if I help you? There's water in the canteen—and it's beautiful up there."

"I can make it, I guess," said the invited guest— the consummate and unblushing hypocrite. Make it he did, with her strong hand to aid; and the glen rang to the laughter of them. While behind them, all unnoted, Johnny Dines reined up on the hillside; took one sweeping glance at that joyous progress, the scarred hillside, the saddle and the dejected eohippus in the background; grinned comprehension, and discreetly withdrew.

45

CHAPTER III

MAXWELTON BRAES

"Oh the song—the song in the blood!
Magic walks the forest; there's bewitchment on the air—
Spring is at the flood!"
                                    —*The Gypsy Heart*

"Well, sir, this here feller, he lit a cigarette an' throwed away the match, an' it fell in a powder kaig; an' do you know, more'n half that powder burned up before they could put it out! Yes, sir!"
                                    —Wildcat Thompson

ELLINOR opened her basket and spread its tempting wares with pretty hostly care—or is there such a word as hostessly?

"There! All ready, Mr.—— I declare, this is too absurd! We don't even know each other's names!" Her conscious eye fell upon the ampleness of the feast —amazing, since it purported to have been put up for one alone; and her face lit up with mischievous de-

46

light. She curtsied. "If you please, I'm the Ultimate Consumer!"

He rose, bowing gravely.

"I am the Personal Devil. Glad to meet you."

"Oh! I've heard of you!" remarked the Ultimate Consumer sweetly. She sat down and extended her hand across the spotless linen. "Mr. Lake says——"

The Personal Devil flushed. It was not because of the proffered hand, which he took unhesitatingly and held rather firmly. The blush was unmistakably caused by anger.

"There is no connection whatever," he stated, grimly enough, "between the truth and Mr. Lake's organs of speech."

"Oh!" cried the Ultimate Consumer triumphantly. "So you're Mr. Beebe?"

"Bransford—Jeff Bransford," corrected the Personal Devil crustily. He wilfully relapsed to his former slipshod speech. "Beebe, he's gone to the Pecos work, him and Ballinger. Mr. John Wesley Also-Ran Pringle's gone to Old Mexico to bring back another bunch of black, long-horned Chihuahuas. You now behold before you the last remaining Rose of Rosebud. But, why Beebe?"

"Why does Mr. Lake hate all of you so, Mr. Bransford?"

"Because we are infamous scoundrels. Why Beebe?"

"I can't eat with one hand, Mr. Bransford," she said demurely. He looked at the prisoned hand with a

47

start and released it grudgingly. "Help yourself," said his hostess cheerfully. "There's sandwiches, and roast beef and olives, for a mild beginning."

"Why Beebe?" he said doggedly.

"Help yourself to the salad and then please pass it over this way. Thank you."

"Why Beebe?"

"Oh, very well then! Because of the little eohippus, you know—and other things you said."

"I see!" said the aggrieved Bransford. "Because I'm not from Ohio, like Beebe, I'm not supposed——"

"Oh, if you're going to be fussy! I'm from California myself, Mr. Bransford. Out in the country at that. Don't let's quarrel, please. We were having such a lovely time. And I'll tell you a secret. It's ungrateful of me, and I ought not to; but I don't care—I don't like Mr. Lake much since we came on this trip. And I don't believe——" She paused, pinkly conscious of the unconventional statement involved in this sudden unbelief.

"——what Lake says about us?" A much-mollified Bransford finished the sentence for her.

She nodded. Then, to change the subject:

"You do speak cowboy talk one minute—and all booky, polite and proper the next, you know. Why?"

"Bad associations," said Bransford ambiguously. "Also for 'tis my nature to, as little dogs they do delight to bark and bite. That beef sure tastes like more."

.   .   .   .

48

"And now you may smoke while I pack up." announced the girl when dessert was over, at long last. "And please, there is something I want to ask you about. Will you tell me truly?"

"Um—you sing?"

"Yes—a little."

"If you will sing for me afterward?"

"Certainly. With pleasure."

"All right, then. What's the story about?"

Ellinor gave him her eyes. "Did you rob the post-office at Escondido—really?"

Now it might be embarrassing to be asked if you had committed a felony; but there was that behind the words of this naïve query—in look, in tone, in mental attitude—an unflinching and implicit faith that, since he had seen fit to do this thing, it must needs have been the right and wise thing to do, which stirred the felon's pulses to a pleasant flutter and caused a certain tough and powerful muscle to thump foolishly at his ribs. The delicious intimacy, the baseless faith, was sweet to him.

"Sure, I did!" he answered lightly. "Lake is one talkative little man, isn't he? Fie, fie! But, shucks! What can you expect? 'The beast will do after his kind.'"

"And you'll tell me about it?"

"After I smoke. Got to study up some plausible excuses, you know."

She studied him as she packed. It was a good face —lined, strong, expressive, vivid; gay, resolute, confident, alert—reckless, perhaps. There were lines of it disused, fallen to abeyance. What was well with the man had prospered; what was ill with him had faded and dimmed. He was not a young man—thirty-seven, thirty-eight—(she was twenty-four)—but there was an unquenchable boyishness about him, despite the few frosty hairs at his temples. He bore his hard years jauntily: youth danced in his eyes. The explorer nodded to herself, well pleased. He was interesting—different.

The tale suffered from Bransford's telling, as any tale will suffer when marred by the inevitable, barbarous modesty of its hero. It was a long story, cozily confidential; and there were interruptions. The sun was low ere it was done.

"Now the song," said Jeff, "and then——" He did not complete the sentence; his face clouded.

"What shall I sing?"

"How can I tell? What you will. What can I know about good songs—or anything else?" responded Bransford in sudden moodiness and dejection—for, after the song, the end of everything! He flinched at the premonition of irrevocable loss.

The girl made no answer. This is what she sang. No; you shall not be told of her voice. Perhaps there is a voice that you remember, that echoes to you through the dusty years. How would you like to describe that?

"Oh, Sandy has monie and Sandy has land,

And Sandy has housen, sae fine and sae grand—
But I'd rather hae Jamie, wi' nocht in his hand,
Than Sandy, wi' all of his housen and land.

"My father looks sulky; my mither looks soor;
They gloom upon Jamie because he is poor.
I lo'e them baith dearly, as a docther should do;
But I lo'e them not half sae weel, dear Jamie, as you!

"I sit at my cribbie, I spin at my wheel;
I think o' the laddie that lo'es me sae weel.
Oh, he had but a saxpence, he brak it in twa,
And he gied me the half o't ere he gaed awa'!

"He said: 'Lo'e me lang, lassie, though I gang awa'!'
He said: 'Lo'e me lang, lassie, though I gang awa'!'
Bland simmer is cooming; cauld winter's awa',
And I'll wed wi' Jamie in spite o' them a'!"

Jeff's back was to a tree, his hat over his eyes. He
pushed it up.

"Thank you," he said; and then, quite directly:
"Are you rich?"

"Not—very," said Ellinor, a little breathless at the
blunt query.

"I'm going to be rich," said Jeff steadily.

" 'I'm going to be a horse,' quoth the little eohippus." The girl retorted saucily, though secretly
alarmed at the import of this examination.

"Ex-actly. So that's settled. What is your name?"
"Hoffman."

"Where do you live, Hoffman?"

"Ellinor," supplemented the girl.

"Ellinor, then. Where do you live, Ellinor?"

"In New York—just now. Not in town. Upstate. On a farm. You see, grandfather's growing old—and he wanted father to come back."

"New York's not far," said Jeff.

A sudden panic seized the girl. What next? In swift, instinctive self-defense she rose and tripped to the tree where lay her neglected sketchbook, bent over—and started back with a little cry of alarm. With a spring and a rush, Jeff was at her side, caught her up and glared watchfully at bush and shrub and tufted grass.

"Mr. Bransford! Put me down!"

"What was it? A rattlesnake?"

"A snake? What an idea! I just noticed how late it was. I must go."

Crestfallen, sheepishly, Mr. Bransford put her down, thrust his hands into his pockets, tilted his chin and whistled an aggravating little trill from the Rye twostep.

"Mr. Bransford!" said Ellinor haughtily.

Mr. Bransford's face expressed patient attention. "Are you lame?"

Mr. Bransford's eye estimated the distance covered during the recent snake episode, and then gave to Miss Hoffman a look of profound respect. His shoulders humped up slightly; his head bowed to the stroke: he stood upon one foot and traced the Rainbow brand in the dust with the other.

"I told you all along I wasn't hurt," he said aggrieved. "Didn't I, now?"

"Are you lame?" she repeated severely, ignoring his truthful saying.

" 'Not—very.' " The quotation marks were clearly audible.

"Are you lame at all?"

"No, ma'am—not what you might call really lame. Uh—no, ma'am."

"And you deceived me like that!" Indignation checked her. "Oh, I am so disappointed in you! That was a fine, manly thing for you to do!"

"It was such a lovely time," observed the culprit doggedly. "And such a chance might never happen again. And it isn't my fault I wasn't hurt, you know. I'm sure I wish I was."

She gave him an icy glare.

"Now see what you've done! Your men haven't come and you won't stay with Mr. Lake. How are you going to get home? Oh, I forgot—you can walk, as you should have done at first."

The guilty wretch wilted yet further. He shuffled his feet; he writhed; he positively squirmed. He ventured a timid upward glance. It seemed to give him courage. Prompted, doubtless, by the same feeling which drives one to dive headlong into dreaded cold water, he said, in a burst of candor:

"Well, you see, ma'am, that little horse now—he really ain't got far. He got tangled up over there a ways——"

The girl wheeled and shot a swift, startled glance at the little eohippus on the hillside, who had long since

53

given over his futile struggles and was now nibbling grass with becoming resignation. She turned back to Bransford. Slowly, scathingly, she looked him over from head to foot and slowly back again. Her expression ran the gamut—wonder, anger, scorn, withering contempt.

"I think I hate you!" she flamed at him.

Amazement triumphed over the other emotions then—a real amazement: the detected impostor had resumed his former debonair bearing and met her scornful eye with a slow and provoking smile.

"Oh, no, you don't," he said reassuringly. "On the contrary, you don't hate me at all!"

"I'm going home, anyhow," she retorted bitterly. "You may draw your own conclusions."

Still, she did not go, which possibly had a confusing effect upon his inferences.

"Just one minute, ma'am, if you please. How did you know so pat where the little black horse was? *I* didn't tell you."

Little waves of scarlet followed each other to her burning face.

"I'm not going to stay another moment. You're detestable! And it's nearly sundown."

"Oh, you needn't hurry. It's not far."

She followed his gesture. To her intense mortification she saw the blue smoke of her home campfire flaunting up from a gully not half a mile away. It was her turn to droop now. She drooped.

There was a painful silence. Then, in a far-off, hard, judicial tone:

"How long, ma'am, if I may ask, have you known that the little black horse was tangled up?"

Miss Ellinor's eyes shifted wildly. She broke a twig from a mahogany bush and examined the swelling buds with minutest care.

"Well?" said her ruthless inquisitor sternly.

"Since—since I went for your hat," she confessed in a half whisper.

"To deceive me so!" Pain, grief, surprise, reproach, were in his words. "Have you anything to say?" he added sadly.

A slender shoe peeped out beneath her denim skirt and tapped on a buried boulder. Ellinor regarded the toetip with interest and curiosity. Then, half-audibly:

"We were having such a good time. . . . And it might never happen again!"

He captured both her hands. She drew back a little —ever so little; she trembled slightly, but her eyes met his frankly and bravely.

"No, no! . . . Not now. . . . Go, now, Mr. Bransford. Go at once. We will have a pleasant day to remember."

"Until the next pleasant day," said resolute Bransford, openly exultant. "But see here, now—I can't go to Lake's camp or to Lake's ball"—here Miss Ellinor pouted distinctly—"or anything that is Lake's. After your masked ball, then what?"

"New York; but it's only so far—on the map." She held her hands apart very slightly to indicate the distance. "On a little map, that is."

"I'll drop in Saturdays," said Jeff.

"Do! I want to hear you sing the rest about the little eohippus."

"If you'll sing about Sandy!" suggested Jeff.

"Why not? Good-by now—I must go."

"And you won't sing about Sandy to any one else?"

The girl considered doubtfully.

"Why—I don't know—I've known you for a very little while, if you please." She gathered up her belongings. "But we're friends?"

"*No! No!*" said Jeff vehemently. "You won't sing it to any one else—Ellinor?"

She drew a line in the dust.

"If you won't cross that line," she said, "I'll tell you."

Mr. Bransford grasped a sapling with a firm clutch and shook it to try its strength.

"A bird in the bush is the noblest work of God," he announced. "I'll take a chance."

Her eyes were shining.

"You've promised!" she said. She paused: when she spoke again her voice was low and a trifle unsteady. "I won't sing about Sandy to—any one else—Jeff!"

Then she fled.

Like Lot's wife, she looked back from the hillside. Jeff clung desperately to the sapling with one hand;

from the other a handkerchief—hers—fluttered a good-by message. She threw him a farewell, with an ambiguous gesture.

. . . .

It was late when Jeff reached Rosebud Camp. He unsaddled Nigger Baby, the little and not entirely gentle black horse, rather unobtrusively; but Johnny Dines sauntered out during the process, announcing supper.

"Huh!" sniffed Jeff. "S'pose I thought you'd wait until I come to get it?"

Nothing more alarming than tallies was broached during supper, however. Afterward, Johnny tilted his chair back and, through cigarette smoke, contemplated the ceiling with innocent eyes.

"Nigger Babe looks drawed," he suggested.

"Uh-huh. Had one of them poor spells of his."

Puff, puff.

"Your saddle's skinned up a heap."

"Run under a tree."

Johnny's look of innocence grew more pronounced.

"How'd you get your clothes so wet?"

"Rain," said Jeff.

Puff, puff.

"You look right muddy too."

"Dust in the air," said Jeff.

"Ah!—yes." Silence during the rolling of another cigarette. Then: "How'd you get that cut on your head?"

Jeff's hand went to his head and felt the bump there. He regarded his fingers in some perplexity.

"That? Oh, that's where I bit myself!" He stalked off to bed in gloomy dignity.

Half an hour later Johnny called softly:

"Jeff!"

Jeff grunted sulkily.

"Camping party down near Mayhill. Lot o' girls. I saw one of 'em. Young person with eyes and hair."

Jeff grunted again. There was a long silence.

"Nice bear!" There was no answer.

"*Good* old bear!" said Johnny tearfully. No answer. "Mister Bear, if I give you one nice, good, juicy bite——"

"*U—ugg—rrh!*" said Jeff.

"Then," said Johnny decidedly, "I'll sleep in the yard.

CHAPTER IV

THE ROAD TO ROME

"Behold, one journeyed in the night.
He sang amid the wind and rain;
My wet sands gave his feet delight—
When will that traveler come again?"
—The Heart of the Road
Anna Hempstead Branch

A HYPOTENUSE, as has been well said, is the longest side of a right-angled triangle. There is no need for details. That we are all familiar with the use of this handy little article is shown by the existence of short-cuts at every available opportunity, and by keep-off-o'-the-grass signs in parks.

Now, had Jeff Bransford desired to go to Arcadia—to that masquerade, for instance—his direct route from Jackson's Ranch would have been cater-cornered across the desert, as has been amply demonstrated by Pythagoras and others.

That Jeff did not want to go to Arcadia—to the masked ball, for instance—is made apparent by the fact that the afternoon preceding said ball saw him jogging southward toward Baird's, along the lonely base of that inveterate triangle whereof Jackson's, Baird's and Arcadia are the respective corners, leaving the fifty-five-mile hypotenuse far to his left. It was also obvious from the tenor of his occasional self-communings.

"I don't want to make a bally fool of myself—do I, old Grasshopper? Anyhow, you'll be too tired when we get to 'Gene's."

Grasshopper made no response, other than a plucky tossing of his bit and a quickening cadence in his rhythmical stride, by way of pardonable bravado.

"I never forced myself in where my company wasn't wanted yet, and I ain't going to begin now," asserted Jeff stoutly; adding, as a fervent afterthought: "Damn Lake!"

His way lay along the plain, paralleling the long westward range, just far enough out to dodge the jutting foothills; through bare white levels where Grasshopper's hoofs left but a faint trace on the hard-glazed earth. At intervals, tempting cross-roads branched away to mountain springs. The cottonwood at Independent Springs came into view round the granite shoulder of Strawberry, six miles to the right of him. He roused himself from prolonged pondering of the marvelous silhouette, where San Andres unflung in broken masses against the sky, to remark in a hushed whisper:

"I wonder if she'd be glad to see me?"

Several miles later he quoted musingly:

"For Ellinor—her Christian name was Ellinor—
Had twenty-seven different kinds of hell in her!"

After all, there are problems which Pythagoras never solved.

The longest road must have an end. Ritch's Ranch was passed far to the right, lying low in the long shadow of Kaylor; then the mouth of Hembrillo Cañon; far ahead, a shifting flicker of Baird's windmill topped the brush. It grew taller; the upper tower took shape. He dipped into the low, mirage-haunted basin, where the age-old Texas Trail crosses the narrow western corner of the White Sands. When he emerged the windmill was tall and silver-shining; the low iron roofs of the house gloomed sullen in the sun.

Dust rose from the corral. Now Jeff's ostensible errand to the West Side had been the search for strays; three days before he had prudently been three days' ride farther to the north. The reluctance with which he had turned back southward was justified by the fact that this critical afternoon found him within striking distance of Arcadia—striking distance, that is, should he care for a bit of hard riding. This exactly what Jeff had fought against all along. So, when he saw the dust, he loped up.

61

It was as he had feared. A band of horses was in the waterpen; among them a red-roan head he knew—Copperhead, of Pringle's mount; confirmed runaway. Jeff shut the gate. For the first time that day, he permitted himself a discreet glance eastward to Arcadia.

"Three days," he said bitterly, while Grasshopper thrust his eager muzzle into the watertrough—"three days I have braced back my feet and slid, like a yearlin' at a brandin' bee—and look at me now! Oh, Copperhead, you darned old fool, see what you done now!"

In this morose mood he went to the house. There was no one at home. A note was tacked on the door.

> Gone to Plomo. Back in two or three days. Beef hangs under platform on windmill tower. When you get it, oil the mill. Books and deck of cards in box under bed. Don't leave fire in stove when you go.
>
> GENE BAIRD.
>
> N. B.—Feed the cat.

Jeff built a fire in the stove and unsaddled the weary Grasshopper. He found some corn, which he put into a woven-grass *morral* and hung on Grasshopper's nose. He went to the waterpen, roped out Copperhead and shut him in a side corral. Then he let the bunch go. They strained through the gate in a mad run, despite shrill and frantic remonstrance from Copperhead.

"Jeff," said Jeff soberly, "are you going to be a damned fool all your life? That girl doesn't care any-

62

thing about you. She hasn't thought of you since. You stay right here and read the pretty books. That's the place for you."

This advice was sound and wise beyond cavil. So Jeff took it valiantly. After supper he hobbled Grasshopper and took off the nosebag. Then he went to the back room in pursuit of literature.

.   .   .   .

Have I leave for a slight digression, to commit a long-delayed act of justice—to correct a grievous wrong? Thank you.

We hear much of Mr. Andrew Carnegie and His Libraries, the Hall of Fame, the Little Red Schoolhouse, the Five-Foot Shelf, and the World's Best Books. A singular thing is that the most effective bit of philanthropy along these lines has gone unrecorded of a thankless world. This shall no longer be.

Know, then, that once upon a time a certain soulless corporation, rather in the tobacco trade, placed in each package of tobacco a coupon, each coupon redeemable by one paper-bound book. Whether they were moved by remorse to this action or by sordid hidden purposes of their own, or, again, by pure, disinterested and farseeing love of their kind, is not yet known; but the results remain. There were three hundred and three volumes on that list, mostly—but not altogether—fiction. And each one was a classic. Classics are cheap. They are not copyrighted. Could I but know the anonymous benefactor who enrolled that glorious company, how gladly would I drop a leaf on his bier or a cherry in his bitters!

Thus it was that, in one brief decade, the cowboys, with others, became comparatively literate. Cowboys all smoked. Doubtless that was a chief cause contributory to making them the wrecks they were. It destroyed their physique; it corroded and ate away their will power—leaving them seldom able to work over nineteen hours a day, except in emergencies; prone to abandon duty in the face of difficulty or danger, when human effort, raised to the nth power, could do no more—all things considered, the most efficient men of their hands on record.

Cowboys all smoked: and the most deep-seated instinct of the human race is to get something for nothing. They got those books. In due course of time they read those books. Some were slow to take to it; but when you stay at lonely ranches, when you are left afoot until the waterholes dry up, so you may catch a horse in the waterpen—why, you must do something. The books were read. Then, having acquired the habit, they bought more books. Since the three hundred and three were all real books, and since the cowboys had been previously uncorrupted of predigested or sterilized fiction, or by "gift," "uplift" and "helpful" books, their composite taste had become surprisingly good, and they bought with discriminating care. Nay, more. A bookcase follows books; a bookcase demands a house; a house needs a keeper; a

64

housekeeper needs everything. Hence alfalfa—house-plants—slotless tables—bankbooks. The chain which began with yellow coupons ends with Christmas trees. In some proudest niche in the Hall of Fame a grateful nation will yet honor that hitherto unrecognized educator, Front de Boeuf.*

.　　.　　.　　.　　.　　.　　.

Jeff pawed over the tattered yellow-backed volumes in profane discontent. He had read them all. Another box was under the bed, behind the first. Opening it, he saw a tangled mass of clothing, tumbled in the bachelor manner; with the rest, a much-used football outfit —canvas jacket, sweater, padded trousers, woolen stockings, rubber noseguard, shinguards, ribbed shoes —all complete; for 'Gene Baird was fullback of the El Paso eleven.

Jeff segregated the gridiron wardrobe with hasty hands. His eye brightened; he spoke in an awed and almost reverent voice.

"I ain't mostly superstitious, but this looks like a leading. First, I'm here; second, Copperhead's here; third, no one else is here; and, for the final miracle, here's a costume made to my hand. Thirty-five miles. Ten o'clock, if I hurry. H'm! 'When first I put this uniform on'—how did that go? I'm forgetting all my songs. Getting old, I guess."

Rejecting the heavy shoes, as unmeet for waxed

* "Bull Durham."

floors, and the shinguards, he rolled the rest of the uniform in his slicker and tied it behind his saddle. Then he rubbed his chin.

"Huh! That's a true saying, too. I am getting old. Youth turns to youth. Buck up, Jeff, you old fool! Have some pride about you and just a little old horse-sense."

Yet he unhobbled Grasshopper, who might then be trusted to find his way to Rainbow in about three days. He went to the corral and tossed a rope on snorting Copperhead. "No; I won't go!" he said, as he slipped on the bridle. "Just to uncock old Copperhead, I'll make a little horseride to Hospital Springs and look through the stock." He threw on the saddle with some difficulty—Copperhead was fat and frisky. "She don't want to see you, Jeff—an old has-been like you! No, no; I'd better not go. I won't! There, if I didn't leave that football stuff on the saddle! I'll take it off. It might get lost. Whoa, Copperhead!"

Copperhead, however, declined to whoa on any terms. His eyes bulged out; he reared, he pawed, he snorted, he bucked, he squealed, he did anything but whoa. Exasperated, Jeff caught the bridle by the cheek piece and swung into the saddle. After a few preliminaries in the pitching line, Jeff started bravely for Hospital Springs.

It was destined that this act of renunciation should be thwarted. Copperhead stopped and dug his feet in the ground as if about to take root. Jeff dug the spurs home. With an agonized bawl, Copperhead made a creditable ascension, shook himself and swapped ends before he hit the ground again. *"Wooh!"* he said. His nose was headed now for Arcadia; he followed his nose, his roan flanks fanned vigorously with a doubled rope.

"Headstrong, stubborn, unmanageable brute! Oh, well, have it your own way then, you old fool! You'll be sorry!" Copperhead leaped out to the loosened rein. "This is just plain kidnapping!" said Jeff.

Kidnapped and kidnapper were far out on the plain as night came on. Arcadia road stretched dimly to the east; the far lights of La Luz flashed through the leftward dusk; straight before them was a glint and sparkle in the sky, faint, diffused, wavering; beyond, a warm and mellow glow broke the blackness of the mountain wall, where the lights of low-hidden Arcadia beat up against Rainbow Rim.

Jeff was past his first vexation; he said as he rode:

"There was ink on her thumb when I kissed her hand,
  And she whispered: 'If you should die
I'd write you an epitaph, gloomy and grand!'
  'Time enough for that!' says I."

"Keep a-movin here, Copperhead! Time fugits right along. You will play hooky, will you? 'I'm going to be a horse!'"

67

CHAPTER V

THE MASKERS

"For Ellinor (her Christian name was Ellinor)
Had twenty-seven different kinds of hell in her."
—Richard Hovey

IT LACKED little of the eleventh hour when the football player reached the ballroom—last comer to the revels. A bandage round his head and a rubber noseguard, which also hid his mouth, served for a mask, eked out by crisscrossed strips of courtplaster. One arm was in a sling—for stage purposes only.

As he limped through the door, Diogenes hurried to meet him, held up his lantern, peered hopefully into the battered face and shook his disappointed head. "Stung again!" muttered Diogenes.

Jeff lisped in numbers which fully verified the cynic's misgiving. "7—11—4—11—44!" he announced jerkily. This strictly in character and

68

also excused him from entangling talk, leaving him free to search the whirl of dancers.

A bulky Rough Rider volunteered his help. He fixed a gleaming eyeglass on his nose and politely offered Jeff a Big Stick by way of a crutch. "Hit the line hard!" he barked. He bit the words off with a prize-bulldog effect. He had fine teeth.

Jeff waved him off. "16—2—1!" he proclaimed controversially. He felt his spirits sinking, with a growing doubt of his ability to identify the Only One, and was impatient of interruption. He kept his slow and watchful way down the floor.

Topsy broke away from her partner and stopped Jeff's crippled progress. Her short hair, braided to a dozen tight and tiny pigtails, bristled away in all directions.

"Laws, young marsta', you suhtenly does look puny!" she said. Then she clutched at her knee. "*Aie!*" she tittered, as a loose red stocking dropped flappingly to her ankle. Pray do not be shocked. The effect was startling; but a black stocking, decorously tight and smooth, was beneath the red one. Jeff's mathematics were not equal to the strain of adequate comment. Topsy dived to the rescue. "Got a string?" she giggled, as she hitched the fallen stocking back to place. "I cain't fix this good nohow!"

Jeff jerked his thumb over his shoulder. "Man over there with an eyeglass cord—maybe you can get that. What makes you act so?" He looked cold disapproval; nevertheless, he looked.

Topsy hung her head, still clutching at the stocking-top. "Dunno. I spec's it's 'cause Ise so wicked!" Finger in mouth, she looked after Jeff as he hobbled away.

A slender witch bounced from a chair and barred his way with a broom. Her eyes were brimming sorcery; her lips looked saucy challenge; she leaned close for a whispered word in his ear: "How would you like to tackle me?"

Poor Jeff! "10, 2—10, 2!" he promised huskily. Yet he ducked beneath the broom.

"But," said the little witch plaintively, "you're going away!" She dropped her broom and wept.

"8, 2—8, 2—8, 2!" said Jeff, almost in tears himself, and again fell back upon English. "Mere figures or mere words can't tell you how much I hate to; but I've got to follow the ball. I'm looking for a fellow."

"If he—if he doesn't love you," sobbed the stricken witch, "then you'll come back to me—won't you? I love a liar!"

"To the very stake!" vowed Jeff. Such heroic, if conditional, constancy was not to go unrewarded. A couple detached themselves from the dancers, threaded their way to a corner of the long hall and stood there in deep converse. Jeff quickened pulse and pace—for one was a Red Devil and the other wore the soft gray costume of a Friend. She was tall, this Quakeress, and the hobnobbing devil was of Jeff's own height. Jeff began to hope for a goal.

Briskly limping, he came to this engrossed couple

and laid a friendly hand on the devil's shoulder.

"Brother," he said cordially, "will you please go to —home?"

The devil recoiled an astonished step.

"What? What!! Show me your license!"

"Twenty-three!—Please!—there's a good devil— 23! I'm the right guard for this lady, I hope. Oh, please to go home!"

The devil took this request in very bad part.

"Go back fifteen yards for offside play and take a drop kick at yourself!" he suggested sourly.

A burly policeman, plainly conscious of fitting his uniform, paused for warning.

"No scrappin' now! Don't start nothin' or I'll run in the t'ree av yees!" he said, and sauntered on, twirling a graceful nightstick.

"Thee is a local man, judging from thy letters," said the Quaker lady, to relieve the somewhat strained situation. "What do they stand for? E. P.? Oh, yes— El Paso, of course!"

"I saw you first!" said the Red Devil. "And with your disposition you would naturally find me more suitable. Make your choice of gridirons! Send him back to the side lines! Disqualify him for interference!"

"Don't be hurried into a decision," said Jeff. "Eternity is a good while. Before it's over I'm going to be a—well, something more than a footballer. Golf, maybe—or tiddledywinks."

The Quakeress glanced attentively from one to the other.

"Doubtless he will do his best to forward Thy Majesty's interests," she interposed. "Why not give him a chance?"

The devil shrugged his shoulders. "I always prefer to give this branch of work my personal attention," he said stiffly.

"A specialty of thine?" mocked the girl.

The devil bowed sulkily.

"My heart is in it. Of course, if you prefer the bungling of a novice, there is no more to be said."

"Thy Majesty's manners have never been questioned," murmured the Quakeress, bowing dismissal. "So kind of you!"

The devil bowed deeply and turned, pausing to hurl a gloomy prophecy over his shoulder. "See you later!" he said, and stalked away with an ill grace.

Pigskin hero and girl Friend, left alone, eyed each other with mutual apprehension. The girl Friend was first to recover speech. Her red lips were prim below her vizor, her eyes downcast to hide their dancing lights. Timidly she spread out fanwise the dove color of her sober costume.

"How does thee like my gray gown?"

"Not at all," said Jeff brutally. "You're no friend of mine, I hope."

A most un-Quakerlike dimple trembled to her chin, relieving the firm austerity of straight lips. Also, Jeff caught a glimpse of her eyes through the vizor. They

72

were crinkling—and they were brown. She ventured another tentative remark, and there was in it an undertone lingering, softly confidential.

"Is thee lame?"

"Not—very," said Jeff, and saw a faint color start to the unmasked moiety of the Quaker cheek. "Still, if I may have the next dance, I shall be glad if you will sit it out with me." Painfully he raised the be-slinged arm in explanation. *Sobre las Olas* throbbed out its wistful call; they set their thought to its haunting measure.

"By all means!" She took his undamaged arm. "Let us find chairs."

Now there were chairs to the left of them, chairs to the right of them, chairs vacant everywhere; but the gallant Six Hundred themselves were not more heedless or undismayed than these two. Still, all the world did not wonder. On the contrary, not even the anxious devil saw them after they passed behind a knot of would-be dancers who were striving to disentangle themselves. For, seeing traffic thus blocked, the policeman rushed to unsnarl the tangle. Magnficently he flourished his stick. He adjured them roughly: "Move on, yous! Move on!" Whereat, with one impulse, the tangle moved on the copper, swept over him, engulfed him, hustled him to the door and threw him out.

So screened, the chair-hunters vanished in far less than a psychological moment: for Jeff, in obedience to a faint or fancied pressure on his arm, dived through portières into a small room set apart for such as had the heart to prefer cards or chess. The room was deserted now and there was a broad window open to the night. Thus, thrice favored of Providence, they found themselves in the garden, chairless but cheerful.

A garden with one Eve is the perfect combination in a world awry. Muffled, the music and the sounds of the ballroom came faint and far to them; star-made shadows danced at their feet. The girl paused, expectant; but it was the unexpected that happened. The nimble tongue which had done such faithful service for Mr. Bransford now failed him quite: left him struggling, dumb, inarticulate, helpless—tongue and hand alike forgetful of their cunning.

Be sure the maid had adoitly heard much of Mr. Bransford, his deeds and misdeeds, during the tedious interval since their first meeting. Report had dwelt lovingly upon Mr. Bransford's eloquence at need. This awkward silence was a tribute of sincerity above question.

With difficulty Ellinor mastered a wild desire to ask where the cat had gone. "Oh, come ye in peace here or come ye in war?" Such injudicious quotation trembled on the tip of her tongue, but she suppressed it—barely in time. She felt herself growing nervous with the fear lest she should be hurried into some all too luminous speech. And still Jeff stood there, lost, speechless, helpless, unready, a clumsy oaf, an object of pity. Pity at last, or a kindred feeling, drove her to

74

the rescue. And, just as she had feared, she said, in her generous haste, far too much.

"I thought you were not coming?"

The inflection made a question of this statement. Also, by implication, it answered so many questions yet unworded that Jeff was able to use his tongue again; but it was not the trusty tongue of yore—witness this wooden speech:

"You mean you thought I said I wasn't coming—don't you? You knew I would come."

"Indeed? How should I know what you would do? I've only seen you once. Aren't you forgetting that?"

"Why else did you make up as a Friend then?"

"Oh! Oh, dear, these men! There's conceit for you! I chose my costume solely to trap Mr. Bransford's eye? Is that it? Doubtless all my thoughts have centered on Mr. Bransford since I first saw him!"

"You know I didn't mean that, Miss Ellinor. I——"

"Miss Hoffman, if you please!"

"Miss Hoffman. Don't be mean to me. I've only got an hour——"

"An hour! Do you imagine for one second—— Why, I mustn't stay here. This is really a farewell dance given in my honor. We go back East day after to-morrow. I must go in."

"Only one little hour. And I have come a long ways for my hour. They take their masks off at midnight—don't they? And of course I can't stay after that. I want only just to ask you——"

"Why did you come then? Isn't it rather unusual to go uninvited to a ball?"

"Why, I reckon you nearly know why I come, Miss Hoffman; but if you want me to say precisely, ma'am——"

"I don't!"

"We'll keep that for a surprise, then. Another thing: I wanted to find out just where you live in New York. I forgot to ask you. And I couldn't very well go round asking folks after you're gone—could I? Of course I didn't have any invitation—from Mr. Lake; but I thought, if he didn't know it, he wouldn't mind me just stepping in to get your address."

"Well, of all the assurance!" said Miss Ellinor. "Do you intend to start up a correspondence with me without even the formality of asking my consent?"

"Why, Miss Ellinor, ma'am, I thought——"

"Miss Hoffman, sir! Yes—and there's another thing. You said you had no invitation—from Mr. Lake. Does that mean, by any chance, that I invited you?"

"You didn't say a word about my coming," said Jeff. He was a flustered man, this poor Bransford, but he managed to put a slight stress upon the word "say."

Miss Ellinor—Miss Hoffman—caught this faint emphasis instantly.

"Oh, I didn't *say* anything? I just looked an invitation, I suppose?" she stormed. "Melting eyes—and that sort of thing? Tears in them, maybe? Poor girl! Poor little child! It would be cruel to let her go home

76

without seeing me again. I will give her a little more happiness, poor thing, and write to her a while. Maybe it would be wiser, though, just to make a quarrel and break loose at once. She'll get over it in a little while after she gets back to New York. Well! Upon my word!"

As she advanced these horrible suppositions, Miss Hoffman had marked out a short beat of garden path —five steps and a turn; five steps back and whirl again—with, on the whole, a caged-tigress effect. With a double-quick at each turn to keep his place at her elbow, Jeff, utterly aghast at the damnable perversity of everything on earth, vainly endeavored to make coördinate and stumbling remonstrance. As she stopped for breath, Jeff heard his own voice at last, propounding to the world at large a stunned query as to whether the abode of lost spirits could afford aught to excel the present situation. The remark struck him: he paused to wonder what other things he had been saying.

Miss Ellinor walked her beat, vindictive. Her chin was at an angle of complacency. She turned up the perky corners of an imaginary mustache with an air, an exasperating little finger, separated from the others, pointing upward in hateful self-satisfaction. Her mouth wore a gratified masculine smirk, visible even in the starlight; her gait was a leisured and lordly strut; her hand waved airy pity. Jeff shrank back in horror.

"M-Miss Hoffman, I n-never d-dreamed——"

Miss Hoffman turned upon him swiftly."

"Never have I heard anything like it—never! You bring me out here willy-nilly, and by way of entertainment you virtually accuse me of throwing myself at your head."

"I never!" said Jeff indignantly. "I didn't——"

Miss Hoffman faced him crouchingly and shook an indictment from her fingers.

"First, you imply that I enticed you to come; second, expecting you, I dressed to catch your eye; third, I was watching eagerly for you——"

"Come—I say now!" The baited and exasperated victim walked headlong into the trap. "The first thing you did was to ask me if I was lame? Wasn't that question meant to find out who I was? When I answered, 'Not—very,' didn't you know at once that it was me?"

"There! That proves exactly what I was just saying," raged the delighted trapper. "You don't even deny it! You say in so many words that I have been courting you! I had to say something—didn't I? You wouldn't! You were limping, so I asked you if you were lame. What else could I have said? Did you want me to stand there like a stuffed Egyptian mummy? That's the thanks a girl gets for trying to help a great, awkward, blundering butter-fingers! Oh, if you could just see yourself! The irresistible conqueror! Not altogether unprincipled though! You *are* capable of compunction. I'll give you credit for that. Alarmed at your easy success, you try to spare me. It is noble of you—noble! You drag me out here, force a quarrel upon me——"

"Oh, by Jove now! Really!" Stung by the poignant injustice of crowding events, Jeff took the bit in his teeth and rushed to destruction. "Really, you must see yourself that I couldn't drag you out here! I have never been in that hall before. I didn't know the lay of the ground. I didn't even know that little side room was there. I thought you pressed my arm a little——" So the brainless colt, in the quicksands, flounders deeper with each effort to extricate himself.

If Miss Hoffman had been angry before she was furious now.

"So *that's* the way of it? Better and better! *I* dragged *you* out! Really, Mr. Bransford, I feel that I should take you back to your chaperon at once. You might be compromised, you know!"

Goaded to desperation, he acted on this hint at once. He turned, with stiff and stilted speech:

"I will take you back to the window, Miss Hoffman. Then there is nothing for me to do but go. I am sorry to have caused you even a moment's annoyance. To-morrow you will see how you have twisted—I mean, how completely you have misinterpreted everything I have said. Perhaps some day you may forgive me. Here is the window. Good-night—good-by!"

Miss Hoffman lingered, however.

"Of course, if you apologize——"

"I do, Miss Hoffman. I beg your pardon most sincerely for anything I have ever said or done that could hurt you in any way."

"If you are sure you are sorry—if you take it all back and will never do such a thing again—perhaps I may forgive you."

"I won't—I am—I will!" said the abject and groveling wretch. Which was incoherent but pleasing. "I didn't mean anything the way you took it; but I'm sorry for everything."

"Then I didn't beguile you to come? Or mask as a Friend in the hope that you would identify me?"

"No, no!"

Miss Ellinor pressed her advantage cruelly. "Nor take stock of each new masker to see if he possibly wasn't the expected Mr. Bransford? Nor drag you into the garden? Nor squeeze your arm?" Her hands went to her face, her lissome body shook. "Oh, Mr. Bransford!" she sobbed between her fingers. "How could you—how *could* you say that?"

The clock chimed. A pealing voice beat out into the night: "Masks off!" A hundred voices swelled the cry; it was drowned in waves of laughter. It rose again tumultuously: *"Masks off! Masks off!"* Nearer came hateful voices, too, that cried: *"Ellinor! Ellinor! Where are you?"*

"I must go!" said Jeff. "They'll be looking for you. No; you didn't do any of those things. You couldn't do any of those things. Good-by!"

"Ellinor! Ellinor Hoffman!! Where are you?"

Miss Hoffman whipped off her mask. From the

80

open window a shaft of light fell on her face. It was flushed, sparkling, radiant. "Masks off!" she said. "Stupid! . . . Oh, you great goose! Of course I did!" She stepped back into the shadow.

No one, as the copybook says justly, may be always wise. Conversely, the most unwise of us blunders sometimes upon the right thing to do. With a glimmer of returning intelligence Mr. Bransford laid his nose-guard on the window-sill.

"*Sir!*" said Ellinor then. "How dare you?" Then she turned the other cheek. "Good-by!" she whispered, and fled away to the ballroom.

Mr. Bransford, in the shadows, scratched his head dubiously.

"Her Christian name was Ellinor," he muttered. "Ellinor! H'm—Ellinor! Very appropriate name. . . . Very! . . . And I don't know yet where she lives!"

He wandered disconsolately away to the garden wall, forgetting the discarded noseguard.

CHAPTER VI

THE ISLE OF ARCADY

"Then the moon shone out so broad and good
    That the barn-fowl crowed:
And the brown owl called to his mate in the wood
    That a dead man lay in the road!"
                                        —Will Wallace Harney

ARCADIA's assets were the railroad, two large modern sawmills, the climate and printer's ink. The railroad found it a patch of bare ground, six miles from water; put in successively a whistling-post, a signboard, a depot, townsite papers and a water-main from the Alamo; and, when the townsite papers were confirmed, established machine shops and made the new town the division headquarters and base for northward building.

The railroad then set up the sawmills, primarily to get out ties and timbers for its own lanky growth, and built a spur to bring the forest down from Rainbow to the mills. The word "down" is used advisedly. Arcadia nestled on the plain under the very eavespouts of Rainbow Range. The branch, following with slavish fidelity the lines of a twisted corkscrew, took twenty-seven miles, mostly tunnel and trestlework, to clamber to the logging camps, with a minimum grade that was purely prohibitive and a maximum that I dare not state; but there was a rise of six thousand feet in those twenty-seven miles. You can figure the average for yourself. And if the engine should run off the track at the end of her climb she would light on the very round-house where she took breakfast, and spoil the shingles.

Yes, that was some railroad. There was a summer hotel—Cloudland—on the summit, largely occupied by slackwire performers. Others walked up or rode a horse. They used stem-winding engines, with eight vertical cylinders on the right side and a shaft like a steamboat, with beveled cogwheel transmission on the axles. And they haven't had a wreck on that branch to date. No matter how late a train is, when an engine sees the tail-lights of her caboose ahead of her she stops and sends out flagmen.

The railroad, under the pseudonym of the Arcadia Development Company, also laid out streets and laid in a network of pipe-lines, and staked out lots until the sawmill protested for lack of tie-lumber. It put down miles of cement walks, fringed them with cotton-wood saplings, telephone poles and electric lights. It built a hotel and a few streets of party-colored cot-

83

tages—directoire, with lingerie tile roofs, organdy façades and peplum, intersecting panels and outside chimneys at the gable ends. It decreed a park, with nooks, lanes, mazes, lake, swans, ballground, grandstand, bandstand and the band appertaining thereunto—all of which apparently came into being over night. Then it employed a competent staff of word-artists and capitalized the climate.

The result was astonishing. The cottonwoods grew apace and a swift town grew with them—swift in every sense of the word. It took good money to buy good lots in Arcadia. People with money must be fed, served and amused by people wanting money. In three years the trees cast a pleasant shade and the company cast a balance, with gratifying results. They discounted the unearned increment for a generation to come.

It was a beneficent scheme, selling ozone and novelty, sunshine and delight. The buyers got far more than the worth of their money, the company got their money—and every one was happy. Health and good spirits are a bargain at any price. There were sand-storms and hot days; but sand promotes digestion and digestion promotes cheerfulness. Heat merely enhanced the luxury of shaded hammocks. As an adventurer thawed out, he sent for seven others worse than himself. Arcadia became the metropolis of the county and, by special election, the county-seat. Courthouse, college and jail followed in quick succession.

For the company, Arcadia life was one grand, sweet song, with, thus far, but a single discord. As has been said, Arcadia was laid out on the plain. There was higher ground on three sides—Rainbow Mountain to the east, the deltas of La Luz Creek and the Alamo to the north and south. New Mexico was dry, as a rule. After the second exception, when enthusiastic citizens went about on stilts to forward a project for changing the town's name to Venice, the company acknowledged its error handsomely. When dry land prevailed once more above the face of the waters, it built a mighty moat by way of the *amende honorable*—a moat with its one embankment on the inner side of the five-mile horseshoe about the town. This, with its attendant bridges, gave to Arcadia an aspect singularly medieval. It also furnished a convenient line of social demarcation. Chauffeurs, college professors, lawyers, gamblers, county officers, together with a few tradesmen and railroad officials, abode within "the Isle of Arcady," on more or less even terms with the Arcadians proper; millmen, railroaders, lumberjacks, and the underworld generally, dwelt without the pale.

The company rubbed its lamp again—and behold! an armory, a hospital and a library! It contributed liberally to churches and campaign funds; it exercised a general supervision over morals and manners. For example, in the deed to every lot sold was an ironclad, fire-tested, automatic and highly constitutional forfeiture clause, to the effect that sale or storage on the premises of any malt, vinous or spirituous liquors

85

should immediately cause the title to revert to the company. The company's own vicarious saloon, on Lot Number One, was a sumptuous and magnificent affair. It was known as The Mint.

All this while we have been trying to reach the night watchman.

In the early youth of Arcadia there came to her borders a warlock Finn, of ruddy countenance and solid build. He had a Finnish name, and they called him Lars Porsena.

Lars P. had been a seafaring man. While spending a year's wage in San Francisco, he had wandered into Arcadia by accident. There, being unable to find the sea, he became a lumberjack—with a custom, when in spirits, of beating the watchman of that date into an omelet.

The indulgence of this penchant gave occasion for much adverse criticism. Fine and imprisonment failed to deter him from this playful habit. One watchman tried to dissuade Lars from his foible with a club, and his successor even went so far as to shoot him—to shoot Lars P., of course, not his predecessor—the successor's predecessor, not Lars Porsena's—if he ever had one, which he hadn't. (What we need is more pronouns.) He—the successor of the predecessor—resigned when Lars became convalescent; but Lars was no whit dismayed by this contretemps—in his first light-hearted moment he resumed his old amusement with unabated gayety.

Thus was one of our greatest railroad systems sub-

jected to embarrassment and annoyance by the idio-
syncrasies of an ignorant but cheerful sailorman. The
railroad resolved to submit no longer to such caprice.
A middleweight of renown was imported, who—when
he was able to be about again—bitterly reproached
the president and demanded a bonus on the ground
that he had knocked Lars down several times before
he—Lars—got angry; and also because of a disquisi-
tion in the Finnish tongue which Lars Porsena had
emitted during the procedure—which address, the
prizefighter stated, had unnerved him and so led to
his undoing. It was obviously, he said, of a nature in-
conceivably insulting; the memory of it rankled yet,
though he had heard only the beginning and did not
get the— But let that pass.

The thing became a scandal. Watchman succeeded
watchman on the company payroll and the hospital
list, until some one hit upon a happy and ingenious
way to avoid this indignity. Lars Porsena was ap-
pointed watchman.

This statesmanlike policy bore gratifying results.
Lars Porsena straightway abandoned his absurd and
indefensible custom, and no imitator arose. Also, Arcadia within the moat—the island—which was the
limit of his jurisdiction, became the most orderly spot
in New Mexico.

.   .   .   .

In the first gray of dawn, Uncle Sam, whistling

down Main Street on his way home from the masquerade, found Lars Porsena lying on his face in a pool of blood.

The belated reveler knelt beside him. The watchman was shot, but still breathed. "Ho! Murder! Help! Murder!" shouted Uncle Sam. The alarm rolled crashing along the quiet street. Heads were thrust from windows; startled voices took up the outcry; other home-goers ran from every corner; hastily arrayed householders poured themselves from street doors.

Lars Porsena was in disastrous plight. He breathed, but that was about all. He was shot through the body. A trail of blood led back a few doors to Lake's Bank. A window was cut out; the blood began at the sill.

Messengers ran to telephone the doctor, the sheriff, Lake. The knot of men grew to a crowd. A rumor spread that there had been an unusual amount of currency in the bank over night—a rumor presently confirmed by Bassett, the bareheaded and white-faced cashier. It was near payday; in addition to the customary amount to cash checks for railroaders and millhands—itself no mean sum—and the money for regular business, there had been provision for contemplated loans to promoters of new local industries.

The doctor came running, made a hasty examination, took emergency measures to stanch the freshly started blood, and swore whole-heartedly at the ambulance and the crowding Arcadians. He administered a stimulant. Lars Porsena fluttered his eyes weakly.

"Stand back, you idiots! Bash these fools' faces in for 'em, some one!" said the medical man. He bent over the watchman. "Who did it, Lars?"

Lars made a vain effort to speak. The doctor gave him another sip of restorative and took a pull himself.

"Try again, old man. You're badly hurt and you may not get another chance. Did you know him?"

Lars gathered all his strength to a broken speech:

"No. . . . Bank. . . . Found window. . . . Midnight . . . nearly. . . . Shot me. . . . Didn't see him." He fell back on Uncle Sam's starry vest.

"Ambulance coming," said Uncle Sam. "Will he live, doc?"

Doc shook his head doubtfully.

"Poor chance. Lost too much blood. If he had been found in time he might have pulled through. Wonderful vitality. Ought to be dead now, by the books. Still, there's a chance."

"I never thought," said Uncle Sam to Cyrano de Bergerac, as the ambulance bore away its unconscious burden, "that I would ever be so sorry at anything that could happen to Lars Porsena—after the way he made me stop singing on my own birthday. He was one grand old fighting machine!"

CHAPTER VII

STATES-GENERAL

"And they hae killed Sir Charlie Hay
And laid the wyte on Geordie."
—Old Ballad

THAT the master's eye is worth two servants had ever been Lake's favorite maxim. He had not yet gone to bed when the message reached him, where he kept his masterly eye on the proper closing up of the ballroom. He came through the crowd now, shouldering his way roughly, still in his police costume—helmet, tunic and belt. In his wake came the sheriff, who had just arrived, scorching to the scene on his trusty wheel.

On the bank steps, Lake turned to face the crowd. His strong canine jaw was set to stubborn fighting lines; the helmet did not wholly hide the black frown or the swollen veins at his temple.

"Come in, Thompson, and help the sheriff size the

thing up—and you, Alec"—he stabbed the air at his choice with a strong blunt finger—"and Turnbull—you, Clarke—and you. . . . Bassett, you keep the door. Admit no one!"

Lake was the local great man. Never had he appeared to such advantage to his admirers; never had his ascendency seemed so unquestioned and so justified. As he stood beside the sheriff in the growing light, the man was the incarnation of power—the power of wealth, position, prestige, success. In this moment of yet unplumbed disaster, taken by surprise, summoned from a night of crowded pleasure, he held his mastery, chose his men and measures with unhesitant decision—planned, ordered, kept to that blunt direct speech of his that wasted no word. A buzz went up from the unadmitted as the door swung shut behind him.

Lake had chosen well. Arcadia in epitome was within those pillaged walls. Thompson was president of the rival bank. Alec was division superintendent. Turnbull was the mill-master. Clarke was editor of the *Arcadian Day*. Clarke had been early to the storm-center; yet, of all the investigators, Clarke alone was not more or less disheveled. He was faultlessly appareled—even to the long Prince Albert and black string tie—in which, indeed, report said, he slept.

So much for capital, industry and the fourth estate. The last of the probers, whom Lake had drafted merely by the slighting personal pronoun "you," was nevertheless identifiable in private life by the name of

91

Billy White—being, indeed, none other than our old friend the devil. His indigenous mustache still retained a Mephistophelian twist; he was becomingly arrayed in slippers, pajamas and a pink bathrobe, girdled at the waist with a most unhermitlike cord, having gone early and surly to bed. In this improvised committee he fitly represented Society: while the sheriff represented society at large and, ex officio, that incautious portion under duress. Yet one element was unrepresented; for Lake made a mistake which other great men have made—of failing to reckon with the masterless men, who dwell without the wall.

Lake led the way.

"Will the watchman die, Alec, d'you think?" whispered Billy, as they filed through the grilled door to the counting room.

"Don't know. Hope not. Game old rooster. Good watchman, too," said Turnbull, the mill-superintendent.

Lake turned on the lights. The wall-safe was blown open; fragments of the door were scattered among the overturned chairs.

In an open recess in the vault there was a dull yellow mass; the explosion had spilled the front rows of coin to a golden heap. Behind, some golden rouleaus were intact: others tottered precariously, as you have perhaps seen beautiful tall stacks of colored counters do. Gold pieces were strewn along the floor.

"Thank God, they didn't get all the gold anyhow!" said Lake, with a sigh of relief. "Then, of course, they didn't touch the silver; but there was a lot of green-backs—over twenty-five thousand, I think. Bassett will know. And I don't know how much gold is gone. Look round and see if they left anything incriminating, sheriff, anything that we can trace them by."

"He heard poor old Lars coming," said the sheriff. "Then, after he shot him, he hadn't the nerve to come back for the gold. This strikes me as being a bungler's job. Must have used an awful lot of dynamite to tear that door up like that! Funny no one heard the explosion. Can't be much of your gold gone, Lake. That compartment is pretty nearly as full as it will hold."

"Or heard him shoot our watchman," suggested Thompson. "Still, I don't know. There's blasting going on in the hills all the time and almost every one was at the masquerade or else asleep. How many times did they shoot old Lars—does anybody know? Is there any idea what time it was done?"

"He was shot once—right here," said Alec, indicating the spot on the flowered silk that had been part of his mandarin's dress. "Gun was held so close it burnt his shirt. Awful hole. Don't believe the old chap'll make it. He crawled along toward the telephone station till he dropped. Say! Central must have heard that shot! It's only two blocks away. She ought to be able to tell what time it was."

"Lars said it was just before midnight," said Clarke.

"Oh!—did he speak?" asked Lake. "How many robbers were there? Did he know any of them?"

"He didn't see anybody—shot just as he reached

93

the window. Hope some one hangs for this!" said Clarke. "Lake, I wish you'd have this money picked up—I'm not used to walking on gold—or else have me watched."

Lake shook his head, angry at the untimely pleasantry. It was a pleasantry in effect only, put forward to hide uneditorial agitation and distress for Lars Porsena. Lake's undershot jaw thrust forward; he fingered the blot of whisker at his ear. It was a time for action, not for talk. He began his campaign.

"Look here, sheriff! You ought to wire up and down the line to keep a lookout. Hold all suspicious characters. Then get a posse to ride for some sign round the town. If we only had something to go on—some clue! Later we'll look through this town with a fine-tooth comb. Most likely they—or he, if there was only one—won't risk staying here. First of all, I've got to telegraph to El Paso for money to stave off a run on the bank. You'll help me, Thompson? Of course my burglar insurance will make good my loss—or most of it; but that'll take time. We mustn't risk a run. People lose their heads so. I'll give you a statement for the *Day*, Clarke, as soon as I find out where Mr. Thompson stands."

"I will back you up, sir. With the bulk of depositors' money loaned out, no bank, however solvent, can withstand a continued run without backing. I shall be glad to tide you over if only for my own protection. A panic is contagious——"

"Thanks," said Lake shortly, interrupting this

94

stately financial discourse. "Then we shall do nicely.
. . . Let's see—to-morrow's payday. You fellows"—
he turned briskly to the two superintendents—"can't
you hold up your payday, say, until Saturday? Stand
your men off. The company stands good for their
money. They can wait a while."

"No need to do that," said Alec. "I'll have the railroad checks drawn on St. Louis. The storekeepers'll
cash 'em. If necessary I'll wire for authority to let
Turnbull pay off the millhands with railroad checks.
It's just taking money from one pocket to put it in
the other, anyhow."

"Then that's all right! Now for the robbers!" The
banker's face betrayed impatience. "My first duty
was to protect my clients; but now we'll waste no
more time. You gentlemen make a close search for any
possible scrap of evidence while the sheriff and I write
our telegrams. I must wire the burglar insurance company, too." He plunged a pen into an inkwell and fell
to work.

Acting upon this hint, the sheriff took a desk. "Wish
Phillips was here—my deputy," he sighed. "I've sent
for him. He's got a better head than I have for noticing
clues and things." This was eminently correct as well
as modest. The sheriff was a Simon-pure Arcadian, the
company's nominee; his deputy was a concession to
the disgruntled Hinterland, where the unobservant
rarely reach maturity.

"Oh, Alec!" said Lake over his shoulder, "you sit
down, too, and wire all your conductors about their

95

passengers last night. Yes, and the freight crews, too. We'll rush those through first. And can't you scare up another operator?" His pen scratched steadily over the paper. "More apt to be some of our local outlaws, though. In that case it will be easier to find their trail. They'll probably be on horseback."

"You were an—old-timer yourself, were you not?" asked Billy amiably. "If the robbers are frontiersmen they may be easier to get track of, as you suggest; but won't they be harder to get?" Billy spoke languidly. The others were searching assiduously for "clues" in the most approved manner, but Billy sprawled easily in a chair.

"We'll get 'em if we can find out who they were," snapped Lake, setting his strong jaw. He did not particularly like Billy—especially since their late trip to Rainbow. "There never was a man yet so good but there was one just a little better."

"By a good man, in this connection, you mean a bad man, I presume?" said Billy in a meditative drawl. "Were you a good man before you became a banker?"

"Look here! What's this?" The interruption came from Clarke. He pounced down between two fragments of the safe door and brought up an object which he held to the light.

At the startled tones, Lake spun round in his swivel-chair. He held out his hand.

"Really, I don't think I ever saw anything like this thing before," he said. "Any of you know what it is?"

"It's a noseguard," said Billy. Billy was a college man and had worn a nosepiece himself. He frowned unconsciously, remembering his successful rival of the masquerade.

"A noseguard? What for?"

"You wear it to protect your nose and teeth when playing football," explained Billy. "Keeps you from swearing, too. You hold this piece between your teeth; the other part goes over your nose, up between your eyes and fastens with this band around your forehead."

"Why! Why!" gasped Clarke, "there was a man at the masquerade togged out as a football player!"

"I saw him," said Alec. "And he wore one of these things. I saw him talking to Topsy."

"One of my guests?" demanded Lake scoffingly. "Oh, nonsense! Some young fellow has been in here yesterday, talking to the clerks, and dropped it. Who went as a football player, White? You know all these college boys. Know anything about this one?"

"Not a thing." There Billy lied—a prompt and loyal gentleman—reasoning that Buttinski, as he mentally styled the interloper who had misappropriated the Quaker lady, would have cared nothing at that time for a paltry thirty thousand. Thus was he guilty of a practice against which we are all vainly warned—of judging others by ourselves. Billy remembered very distinctly that Miss Ellinor had not reappeared until the midnight unmasking, and he therefore acquitted her companion of this particular crime,

97

entirely without prejudice to Buttinski's felonious instincts in general. For the watchman had been shot before midnight. Billy made a tentative mental decision that this famous noseguard had been brought to the bank later and left there purposely; and resolved to keep his eye open.

"Oh, well, it's no great difference anyhow," said Lake. "Whoever it was dropped it here yesterday, I guess, and got another one for the masquerade."

"Hold on there!" said Clarke, holding the spotlight tenaciously. "That don't go! This thing was on top of one of those pieces of the safe!"

For the first time Lake was startled from his iron composure.

"Are you sure?" he demanded, jumping up.

"Sure! It was right here against the sloping side of this piece—so."

"That puts a different light on the case, gentlemen," said Lake. "Luck is with us; and——"

"And, while I think of it," said Clarke, making the most of his unexpected opportunity, "I made notes of all the costumes and their wearers after the masks were off—for the paper, you know—and I saw no football player there. I remember that distinctly."

"I only saw him the one time," confirmed Alec, "and I stayed almost to the break-up. Whoever it was, he left early."

"But what possible motive could the robber have for going to the dance at all?" queried Lake in perplexity.

"Maybe he made his appearance there in a football suit purposely, so as to leave us some one to hunt for, and then committed the robbery and went back in another costume," suggested Clarke, pleased and not a little surprised at his own ingenuity. "In that case, he would have left this rubber thing here of design."

"H'm!" Lake was plainly struck with this theory. "And that's not such a bad idea, either! We'll look into this football matter after breakfast. You'll go to the hotel with me, gentlemen? Our womankind are all asleep after the ball. The sheriff will send some one to guard the bank. Meantime I'll call the cashier in and find out exactly how much money we're short. Send Bassett in, will you, Billy? You stay at the door and keep that mob out."

CHAPTER VIII

ARCADES AMBO

"What means this, my lord?"
"Marry, this is miching mallecho; it means mischief."
                                                    —*Hamlet*

"We are here to do what service we may, for honor and not for
hire."   —Robert Louis Stevenson

WITH Billy went the sheriff and Alec, the latter with
a sheaf of telegrams.

"Now . . . how did Buttinski's noseguard get into
this bank? That's what I'd like to know," said Billy
to the doorknob, when the other committeemen had
gone their ways. "I didn't bring it. I don't believe
Buttinski did. . . . And Policeman Lake certainly saw
us quarreling. He noticed the football player, right
enough,—and he pretends he didn't. Why—why—
why does Policeman Lake pretend he didn't see that

football player? Echo answers—why? . . . Denmark's all putrefied!"

The low sun cleared the housetops. The level rays fell along the window-sill; and Billy, staring fascinated at the single blotch of dried blood on the inner sill, saw something glitter and sparkle there beside it. He went closer. It was a dust of finely powdered glass. Billy whistled.

A light foot ran up the steps. There was a rap at the door.

"No entrance except on business. No business transacted here!" quoted Billy, startled from a deep study. A head appeared at the window. "Oh, it's you, Jimmy? That's different. Come in!"

It was Jimmy Phillips, the chief deputy. Billy knew him and liked him. He unbarred the door.

"Well, anything turned up yet?" demanded Jimmy. "I stopped in to see Lars. Him and me was old side partners."

"How's he making it, Jimmy?"

"Oh, doc said he had one chance in ten thousand; so he's all right, I guess," responded that brisk optimist. "They got any theory about the robber?"

"They have that. A perfectly sound theory, too— only it isn't true," said Billy in a low and guarded tone. "They'll tell you. I haven't got time. See here—if I give you the straight tip will you work it up and keep your head closed until you see which way the cat jumps? Can you keep it to yourself?"

"Mum as a sack of clams!" said Jimmy.

"Look at this a minute!" Billy pointed to the tiny particles of glass on the inner sill. "Got that? Then I'll dust it off. This is a case for your gummiest shoes. Now look at this!" He indicated the opening where the patch of glass had been cut from the big pane. Jimmy rubbed his finger very cautiously along the raw edge of the glass.

"Cut out from the inside—then carried out there? A frame-up?"

"Exactly. But I don't want anybody else to size it up for a frame-up—not now."

"But," said Jimmy good-naturedly, "I'd 'a' seen all that myself after a little if you hadn't 'a' showed me."

"Yes," said Billy dryly; "and then told somebody! That's why I brushed the glass-dust off. I've got inside information—some that I'm going to share with you and some that I am not going to tell even you!"

"Trot it out!"

"Lake had the key of this front door in the policeman's uniform that he wore to the dance. Isn't that queer? If I were you I'd very quietly find out whether he went home to get that key after he got word that the bank was robbed. He was still in the ballroom when he got the message."

"You think it's a put-up job? Why?"

"There is something not just right about the man Lake. His mind is too ballbearing altogether. He herds those chumps in there round like so many sheep. He used 'em to make discoveries with and then showed 'em how to force 'em on him. Oh, they made a heap of

102

progress! They've got evidence enough up in there to hang John the Baptist, with Lake all the time setting back in the breeching like a balky horse. It's Lake's bank, and the bank's got burglar insurance. Got that? If he gets the money and the insurance, too—see? And I happen to know he has been bucking the market. I dropped a roll with him myself. Then there's r-r-revenge!—as they say on the stage—and something else beside. Has Lake any bitter enemies?"

"Oodles of 'em!"

"But one worse than the others—one he hates most?"

Jimmy thought for a while. Then he nooded.

"Jeff Bransford, I reckon."

"Is he in town?"

"Not that I know of."

"Well, I never heard of your Mr. Bransford; but he's in town all right, all right! You'll see! Lake's got a case cooked up that'll hang some one higher than Haman; and I'll bet the first six years of my life against a Doctor Cook lecture ticket that the first letter of some one's name is Jeff Bransford."

"Maybe Jeff can prove he was somewhere else?" suggested Jimmy.

Billy evaded the issue.

"What sort of a man is this Bransford? Any good? Besides being an enemy of Lake's, I mean?"

"Mr. Bransford is one whom we all delight to humor," announced the deputy, after some reflection.

"Friend of yours?"

103

Jimmy reflected again.

"We-ll—yes!" he said. "He limps a little in cold weather, and I got a little small ditch plowed in my skull—but our horses was both young and wild, and the boys rode in between us before there was any harm done. I pulled him out of the Pecos since that, too, and poured some several barrels of water out o' him. Yes, we're good friends, I reckon."

"He'll shoot back on proper occasion, then? A good sport? Stand the gaff?"

"On proper occasion," rejoined Jimmy, "the other man will shoot back—if he's lucky. Yes, sir, Jeff's certainly one dead game sport at any turn in the road."

"Considering the source and spirit of your information, you sadden me," said Billy. "The better man he is, the better chance to hang. Has he got any close friends here?"

"He seldom ever comes here," said Jimmy. "All his friends is on Rainbow, specially South Rainbow; but his particular side partners is all away just now; leastways, all but one."

"Can't you write to that one?"

The deputy grinned hugely.

"And tell him to come break Jeff out o' jail?" said he. "That don't seem hardly right, considerin'. You write to him—Johnny Dines, Morningside. You might wire up to Cloudland and have it forwarded from there. I'll pay."

Billy made a note of it.

"They'll be out here in a jiffy now," he said. "Now,

Jimmy, you listen to all they tell you; follow it up; make no comments; don't see anything and don't miss anything. Let Lake think he's having it all his own way and he'll make some kind of a break that will give him away. We haven't got a thing against him yet except the right guess. And you be careful to catch your friend without a fight. When you get him I want you to give him a message from me; but don't mention any name. Tell him to keep a stiff upper lip—that the devil takes care of his own. Say the devil told you himself—in person. I don't want to show my hand. I'm on the other side—see? That way I can be in Lake's counsels—force myself in, if necessary, after this morning."

"You think that if you give Lake rope enough——"

"Exactly. Here they come—I hear their chairs."

"Blonde or brunette?" said Jimmy casually.

"Eh? What's that?"

"The something else that you wouldn't tell me about," Jimmy explained. "Is she blonde or brunette?"

"Oh, go to hell!" said Billy.

CHAPTER IX

TAKEN

"Lord Huntley then he did speak out—
 O, fair mot fa' his body!—
'I here will fight doublet alane
 Or ony thing ails Geordie!

'Whom has he robbed? What has he stole?
 Or has he killed ony?
Or what's the crime that he has done
 His foes they are so mony?'"
                                        —Old Ballad

HUE AND CRY, hubbub and mystery, swept the Isle of Arcady that morning, but the most painstaking search and query proved fruitless. It developed beyond doubt that the football man had not been seen since his one brief appearance on the ballroom floor. Search was transferred to the mainland, where, as it neared noon, Lake's perseverance and thoroughness were rewarded. In Chihuahua suburb, beyond the north wall, Lake noted a sweat-marked, red-roan horse in the yard of Rosalio Marquez, better known, by reason of his profession, as Monte.

Straightway the banker reported this possible clue to the sheriff and to Billy, who was as tireless and determined in the chase as Lake himself. The other masqueraders had mostly abandoned the chase. He found them on the bridge of the La Luz sallyport.

"It may be worth looking into," Lake advised the sheriff. "Better send some one to reconnoiter—some one not known to be connected with your office. You go, Billy. If you find anything suspicious the sheriff can 'phone to the hospital if he needs me. I'm going over to see how the old watchman is—ought to have gone before. If he gets well I must do something handsome for him."

Billy fell in with this request. He had a well-founded confidence in Lake's luck and attached much more significance to the trifling matter of the red-roan horse than did the original discoverer—especially since the discoverer had bethought himself to go to the hospital on an errand of mercy. Billy now confidently expected early developments. And he preferred personally to conduct the arrest, so that he might interfere, if necessary, to prevent any wasting of good cartridges. He did not expect much trouble, however, providing the affair was conducted tactfully; reasoning that a dead game sport with a clean conscience and a light heart would not seriously object to a small arrest. Poor Billy's own heart was none of the lightest as he went on this loyal service to his presumably favored rival.

Bicycle-back, he accompanied the sheriff beyond the outworks to the Mexican quarter. Near the place indicated by the banker Billy left his wheel and strolled casually round the block. He saw the red-roan steed and noted the Double Rainbow branded on his thigh.

Monte was leaning in the adobe doorway, rolling a cigarette. Billy knew him, in a business way.

"Hello, Monte! Good horse you've got there."

"Yais—tha's nice hor-rse," said Monte.

"Want to sell him?"

"Thees ees not my hor-rse," explained Monte. "He ees of a frien'."

"I like his looks," said Billy. "Is your friend here? Or, if he's downtown, what's his name? I'd like to buy that horse."

"He ees weetheen, but he ees not apparent. He ees *dormiendo*—ah—yais—esleepin'. He was las' night to the *baile mascarada*."

Billy nodded. "Yes; I was there myself." He decided to take a risk: assuming that his calculations were correct, x must equal Bransford. So he said carelessly: "Let's see, Bransford went as a sailor, didn't he? *Un marinero?*"

"Oh, no; he was atir-re' lak one—*que cosa?*—what you call thees theeng?—*un balon para jugar con los pies?* Ah! si, si!—one feetball! Myself I come soon back. I have no beesness. The bes' people ees all for

108

the dance," said Monte, with hand turned up and shrugging shoulder. "So, *media noche*—twelve of the clock, I am here back. I fin' here the hor-rse of my frien', and one *carta*—letter—that I am not to lock the door; *porque* he may come to esleep. So I am mek to r-repose myself. Later I am ar-rouse when my frien' am to r-retir-re heemself. Oh, *que hombre!* I am yet to esmile to see heem in thees so r-redeeculous *vestidos!* He ees ver' gay. Ah! *que* Jeff! Een all ways thees ees a man ver' *suficiente*, cour-rageous, es-trong, formidabble! Yet he ees keep the *disposicion*, the hear-rt, of a simple leetle chil'—*un muchacho!*"

"I'll come again," said Billy, and passed on. He had found out what he had come for. The absence of concealment dispelled any lingering doubt of Jeff Buttinski. Yet he could establish no alibi by Monte.

Perhaps Billy White may require here a little explanation. All things considered, Billy thought Jeff would be better off in jail, with a friend in the opposite camp working for his interest, than getting himself foolishly killed by a hasty posse. If we are cynical, we may say that, being young, Billy was not averse to the rôle of *deus ex machina*; perhaps a thought of friendly gratitude was not lacking. Then, too, adventure for adventure's sake is motive enough—in youth. Or, as a final self-revelation, we may hint that if Jeff was a rival, so too was Lake—and one more eligible. Let us not be cynical, however, or cowardly. Let us say at once shamelessly what we very well know— that youth is the season for clean honor and high emprise; that boy's love is best and truest of all; that poor, honest Billy, in his own dogged and fantastic way, but sought to give true service where he—loved. There, we have said it; and we are shamed. How old are you, sir? Forty? Fifty? Most actions are the result of mixed motives, you say? Well, that is a notable concession—at your age. Let it go at that. Billy, then, acted from mixed motives.

When Billy brought back his motives—and the sheriff—Monte still held his negligent attitude in the doorway. He waved a graceful salute.

"I want to see Bransford," said the sheriff.

"He ees esleepin'," said Monte.

"Well, I want to see him anyway!" The sheriff laid a brisk hand on the gatelatch.

Monte waved his cigarette airily, flicked the ash from the end with a slender finger, and once more demonstrated that the hand is quicker than the eye. The portentously steady gun in the hand was the first intimation to the eye that the hand had moved at all. It was a very large gun as to caliber, the sheriff noted. As it was pointed directly at his nose he was favorably situated to observe—looking along the barrel—that the hammer stood at full cock.

"Per-rhaps you have some papers for heem?" suggested Monte, with gentle and delicate deference. He still leaned against the doorjamb. "But eef not eet ees bes' that you do not enter thees my leetle house to distur-rb my gues'. That would be to commeet a r-rudeness—no?"

110

The sheriff was a sufficiently brave man, if not precisely a brilliant one. Yet he showed now intelligence of the highest order. He dropped the latch.

"You Billy, stop your laughing! Do you know, Mr. Monte, I think you are quite right?" he observed, with a smiling politeness equal to Monte's own. "That would be rude, certainly. My mistake. An Englishman's house is his castle—that sort of thing? If you will excuse me now we will go and get the papers, as you so kindly pointed out."

They went away, the sheriff, Billy and motives— Billy still laughing immoderately.

Monte went inside and stirred up his guest with a prodding boot-toe.

"Meester Jeff," he demanded, "what you been a-doin' now?"

Jeff sat up, rumpled his hair, and rubbed his eyes. "Sleepin'," he said.

"An' before? *Porque*, the sheriff he has been. To mek an arres' of you, I t'eenk."

"Me?" said Jeff, rubbing his chin thoughtfully. "I haven't done anything that I can remember now!"

"Sure? No small leetle cr-rime? Not las' night? Me, I jus' got up. I have not hear'."

Jeff considered this suggestion carefully. "No. I am sure. Not for years. Some mistake, I guess. Or maybe he just wanted to see me about something else. Why didn't he come in?"

"I mek r-reques' of heem that he do not," said Monte.

"I see," Jeff laughed. "Come on; we'll go see him. You don't want to get into trouble."

They crossed the bridge and met the sheriff just within the fortifications, returning in a crowded automobile. Jeff held up his hand. The machine stopped and the posse deployed—except Billy, who acted as chauffeur.

"You wanted to see me, sheriff—at the hotel?"

"Why, yes, if you don't mind," said the sheriff.

"Good dinner? I ain't had breakfast yet!"

"First-class," said the sheriff cordially. "Won't your friend come too?"

"Ah, señor, you eshame me that I am not so hospitabble, ees eet not?" purred Monte, as he followed Jeff into the tonneau.

The sheriff reddened and Billy choked.

"Nothing of the sort," said the sheriff hastily, lapsing into literalness. "You were quite within your rights. For that matter, I know you were at your own bank, dealing, when the crime was committed. I am holding you for the present as a possible accessory; and, if not, then as a material witness. By the way, Monte, would you mind if I sent some men to look through your place? There is a matter of some thirty thousand dollars missing. Lake asked us to look for it. I have papers for it if you care to see them."

"Oh, no, señor!" said Monte. He handed over a key. "*La casa es suyo!*"

"Thank you," said the sheriff, with unmoved

112

gravity. "Anything of yours you want 'em to bring, Bransford?"

"Why, no," said Jeff cheerfully. "I've got nothing there but my saddle, my gun and an old football suit that belongs to 'Gene Baird, over on the West Side; but if you want me to stay long, I wish you'd look after my horse."

"I too have lef' there my gun that I keep to protec' my leetle house," observed Monte. "Tell some one to keep eet for me. I am much attach' to that gun."

"Why, yes, I have seen that gun, I think," said the sheriff. "They'll look out for it. All right, Billy!"

The car turned back.

"Oh—you were speaking about Monte being an accessory. I didn't get in till 'way late last night, and I've been asleep all day," said Jeff apologetically. "Might I ask before or after exactly what fact Monte was an accessory?"

"Bank robbery, for one thing."

"Ah! . . . That would be Lake's bank? Anything else?"

The sheriff was not a patient man and he had borne much; also, he liked Lars Porsena. Perfection, even in trifles, is rare and wins affection. He turned on Jeff, with an angry growl.

"Murder!"

"Lake?" murmured Jeff hopefully.

The sheriff continued, ignoring and, indeed, only half sensing the purport of Jeff's comment:

"At least, the wound may not be mortal."

"That's too bad," said Jeff. He was, if possible, more cheerful than ever.

The sheriff glared at him. Billy, from the front seat, threw a word of explanation over his shoulder. "It's not Lake. The watchman."

"Oh, old Lars Porsena? That's different. Not a bad sort, Lars. Maybe he'll get well. Hope so. . . . And I shot him? Dear me! When did it happen?"

"You'll find out soon enough!" said the sheriff grimly. "Your preliminary's right away."

"Hell, I haven't had breakfast yet!" Jeff protested. "Feed us first or we won't be tried at all."

·   ·   ·   ·   ·   ·   ·

Within the jail, while the sheriff spoke with his warder, it occurred to Billy that, since Jimmy Phillips was not to be seen, he might as well carry his own friendly message. So he said guardedly:

"Buck up, old man! Keep a stiff upper lip and be careful what you say. This is only your preliminary trial, remember. Lots of things may happen before court sets. The devil looks after his own, you know."

Jeff had a good ear for voices, however, and Billy's mustache still kept more than a hint of Mephistoph- eles. Jeff slowly surveyed Billy's natty attire, with a lingering and insulting interest for such evidences of prosperity as silken hosiery and a rather fervid scarf- pin. At last his eye met Billy's, and Billy was blushing.

114

"Does he?" drawled Jeff languidly. "Ah! . . . You own the car, then?"

Poor Billy!

Notwithstanding the ingratitude of this rebuff, Billy sought out Jimmy Phillips and recounted to him the circumstances of the arrest.

"Oh, naughty, naughty!" said the deputy, caressing his nose. "Lake's been a cowman on Rainbow. He knew the brand on that horse; he knew Jeff was chummy with Monte. He knew in all reason that Jeff was in there, and most likely he knew it all the time. So he sneaks off to see Lars—after shooting him from ambush, damn him!—and sends you to take Jeff. Looks like he might be willing for you and Jeff to damage either, which or both of yourselves, as the case may be."

"It looks so," said Billy.

"Must be a fine girl!" murmured Jimmy absently. "Well, what are you going to do? It looks pretty plain."

"It looks plain to us—but we haven't got a single tangible thing against Lake yet. We'd be laughed out of court if we brought an accusation against him. We'll have to wait and keep our eyes open."

"You're sure Lake did it? There was no rubber nosepiece at Monte's house. All the rest of the football outfit—but not that. That looks bad for Jeff."

"On the contrary, that is the strongest link against Lake. I dare say Buttinski—Mr. Bransford—is eminently capable of bank robbery at odd moments; but

I know approximately where that noseguard was at sharp midnight—after the watchman was shot." Here Billy swore mentally, having a very definite guess as to how Jeff might have lost the noseguard. "Lake, Clarke, Turnbull, Thompson, Alec or myself—one of the six of us—brought that noseguard to the bank after the robbery, and only one of the six had a motive —and a key."

"Only one of you had a key," corrected Jimmy cruelly. "But can't Jeff prove where he was, maybe?"

"He won't."

"I'd sure like to see her," said Jimmy.

CHAPTER X

THE ALIBI

"And all love's clanging trumpets shocked and blew."

"The executioner's argument was, that you couldn't cut off a head unless there was a body to cut it off from; that he had never had to do such a thing before, and he wasn't going to begin at *his* time of life."   —Alice in Wonderland

THE justice of the peace, when the county court was not in session, held hearings in the courtroom proper, which occupied the entire second story of the county courthouse. The room was crowded. It was a new courthouse; there are people impatient to try even a new hearse; and this bade fair to be Arcadia's first *cause célèbre*.

Jeff sat in the prisoner's stall, a target for boring eyes. He was conscious of an undesirable situation; exactly how tight a place it was he had no means of

117

knowing until he should have heard the evidence. The room was plainly hostile; black looks were cast upon him. Deputy Phillips, as he entered arm in arm with the sometime devil, gave the prisoner an intent but non-committal look, which Jeff rightly interpreted as assurance of a friend in ambush; he felt unaccountably sure of the devil's fraternal aid; Monte, lolling within the rail of the witness-box, smiled across at him. Still, he would have felt better for another friendly face or two, he thought—say, John Wesley Pringle's.

Jeff looked from the open window. Cottonwoods, well watered, give swiftest growth of any trees and are therefore the dominant feature of new communities in dry lands. The courthouse yard was crowded with them: Jeff, from the window, could see nothing but their green plumes; and his thoughts ran naturally upon gardens—or, to be more accurate, upon a garden.

Would she lose faith in him? Had she heard yet? Would he be able to clear himself? No mere acquittal would do. Because of Ellinor, there must be no question, no verdict of Not Proven. She would go East tomorrow. Perhaps she would not hear of his arrest at all. He hoped not. The bank robbery, the murder— yes, she would hear of them, perhaps; but why need she hear his name? Hers was a world so different! He fell into a muse at this.

Deputy Phillips passed and stood close to him, looking down from the window. His back was to Jeff; but, under cover of the confused hum of many voices, he spake low from the corner of his mouth:

"Play your hand close to your bosom, old-timer! Wait for the draw and watch the dealer!" He strolled over to the other side of the judicial bench whence he came.

This vulgar speech betrayed Jimmy as one given to evil courses; but to Jeff that muttered warning was welcome as thunder of Blücher's squadrons to British squares at Waterloo.

Down the aisle came a procession consciously important—the prosecuting attorney; the bank's lawyer, who was to assist, "for the people"; and Lake himself. As they passed the gate Jeff smiled his sweetest.

"Hello, Wally!" Lake's name was Stephen Walter.

Wally made no verbal response; but his undershot jaw did the steel-trap act and there was a triumphant glitter in his eye. He turned his broad back pointedly —and Jeff smiled again.

The justice took his seat on the raised dais intervening between Jeff and the sheriff's desk. Court was opened. The usual tedious preliminaries followed. Jeff waived a jury trial, refused a lawyer and announced that he would call no witnesses at present.

In an impressive stillness the prosecutor rose for his opening statement. Condensed, it recounted the history of the crime, so far as known; fixed the time by the watchman's statement—to be confirmed, he said, by another witness, the telephone girl on duty at that hour, who had heard the explosion and the ensuing gunshot; touched upon that watchman's faithful service and his present desperate condition. He told of the late finding of the injured man, the meeting in the bank, the sum taken by the robber, and the discovery in the bank of the rubber nosepiece, which he submitted as Exhibit A. He cited the witnesses by whom he would prove each statement, and laid special stress upon the fact that the witness Clarke would testify that the nosepiece had been found upon the shattered fragments of the safe door—conclusive proof that it had been dropped after the crime. And he then held forth at some length upon the hand of Providence, as manifested in the unconscious self-betrayal which had frustrated and brought to naught the prisoner's fiendish designs. On the whole, he spoke well of Providence.

Now Jeff had not once thought of the discarded noseguard since he first found it in his way; he began to see how tightly the net was drawn round him. "There was a serpent in the garden," he reflected. A word from Miss Hoffman would set him free. If she gave that word at once, it would be unpleasant for her: but if she gave it later, as a last resort, it would be more than unpleasant. And in that same hurried moment, Jeff knew that he would not call upon her for that word. All his crowded life, he had kept the happy knack of falling on his feet: the stars, that fought in their courses against Sisera, had ever fought for reckless Bransford. He decided, with lovable folly, to trust to chance, to his wits and to his friends.

120

"And now, Your Honor, we come to the unbreakable chain of evidence which fatally links the prisoner at the bar to this crime. We will prove that the prisoner was not invited to the masquerade ball given last night by Mr. Lake. We will prove——"

There was a stir in the courtroom; the prosecutor paused, disconcerted. Eyes were turned to the double door at the back of the courtroom. In the entryway at the head of the stairs huddled a group of shrinking girls. Before them, one foot upon the threshold, stood Ellinor Hoffman. She shook off a detaining hand and stepped into the room, head erect, proud, pale. Across the sea of curious faces her eyes met the prisoner's. Of all the courtroom, Billy and Deputy Phillips alone turned then to watch Jeff's face. They saw an almost imperceptible shake of his head, a finger on lip, a reassuring gesture—saw, too, the quick pulsebeat at his throat.

The color flooded back to Ellinor's face. Men nearest the door were swift to bring chairs. The prosecutor resumed his interrupted speech—his voice was deep, hard, vibrant.

"Your Honor, the counts against this man are fairly damning! We will prove that he was shaved in a barber shop in Arcadia at ten o'clock last night; that he then rode a roan horse; that the horse was then sweating profusely; that this horse was afterward found at the house of—but we will take that up later. We will prove by many witnesses that among the masqueraders was a man wearing a football suit, wearing

121

a nosepiece similar—entirely similar—to the one found in the bank, which now lies before you. We will prove that this football player was not seen in the ballroom after the hour of eleven P.M. We will prove that when he was next seen, without the ballroom, it was not until sufficient time had elapsed for him to have committed this awful crime."

Ellinor half rose from her seat; again Jeff flashed a warning at her.

"We will prove this, Your Honor, by a most unwilling witness—Rosalio Marquez"—Monte smiled across at Jeff—"a friend of the prisoner, who, in his behalf, has not scrupled to defy the majesty of the law! We can prove by this witness, this reluctant witness, that when he returned to his home, shortly after midnight, he found there the prisoner's horse, which had not been there when Mr. Marquez left the house some four hours previously: and that, at some time subsequent to twelve o'clock, the witness Marquez was wakened by the entrance of the prisoner at the bar, clad in a football suit, but wearing no nosepiece with it! And we have the evidence of the sheriff's posse that they found in the home of the witness, Rosalio Marquez, the football suit—which we offer as Exhibit B. Nay, more! The prisoner did not deny, and indeed admitted, that this uniform was his; but—mark this! —the searching party found no nosepiece there!

"It is true, Your Honor, that the stolen money was not found upon the prisoner; it is true that the prisoner made no use of the opportunity to escape offered

122

him by his lawless and disreputable friend, Rosalio Marquez—a common gambler! Doubtless, Your Honor, his cunning had devised some diabolical plan upon which he relied to absolve himself from suspicion; and now, trembling, he has for the first time learned of the fatal flaw in his concocted defense, which he had so fondly deemed invincible!"

All eyes, including the orator's, here turned upon the prisoner—to find him, so far from trembling, quite otherwise engaged. The prisoner's elbow was upon the rail, his chin in his hand; he regarded Mr. Lake attentively, with cheerful amusement and a quizzical smile which in some way subtly carried an expression of mockery and malicious triumph. To this fixed and disconcerting regard Mr. Lake opposed an iron front, but the effort required was apparent to all.

There was an uneasy rustling through the court. The prisoner's bearing was convincing, natural; this was no mere brazen assuming. The banker's forced composure was not natural! He should have been an angry banker. Of the two men, Lake was the less at ease. The prisoner's face turned at last toward the door. Blank unrecognition was in his eyes as they swept past Ellinor, but he shook his head once more, very slightly.

There was a sense of mystery in the air—a buzz and burr of whispers; a rustle of moving feet. The audience noticeably relaxed its implacable attitude toward the accused, eyed him with a different interest, seemed to feel for the first time that, after all, he was accused merely, and that his defense had not yet been heard. The prosecutor felt this subtle change; it lamed his periods.

"It is true, Your Honor, that no eye save God's saw this guilty man do this deed; but the web of circumstantial evidence is so closely drawn, so far-reaching, so unanswerable, so damning, that no defense can avail him except the improbable, the impossible establishment of an alibi so complete, so convincing, as to satisfy even his bitterest enemy! We will ask you, Your Honor, when you have seen how fully the evidence bears out our every contention, to commit the prisoner, without bail, to answer the charge of robbery and attempted murder!"

Then, by the door, Jeff saw the girl start up. She swept down the aisle, radiant, brave, unfearing, resolute, all half-gods gone; she shone at him—proud, glowing, triumphant!

A hush fell upon the thrilled room. Jeff was on his feet, his hand held out to stay her; his eyes spoke to hers. She stopped as at a command. Scarcely slower, Billy was at her side. "Wait! Wait!" he whispered. "See what he has to say. There will be always time for that." Jeff's eyes held hers; she sank into an offered chair.

Cheated, disappointed, the court took breath again. Their dramatic moment had been nothing but their own nerves; their own excited imaginings had attached a pulse-fluttering significance to the flushed cheeks of a prying girl, seeking a better place to see and hear, to gratify her morbid curiosity.

Jeff turned to the bench.

"Your Honor, I have a perfectly good line of defense; and I trust no friend of mine will undertake to change it. I will keep you but a minute," he said colloquially. "I will not waste your time combating the ingenious theory which the prosecution has built up, or in cross-examination of their witnesses, who, I feel sure"—here he bowed to the cloud of witnesses—"will testify only to the truth. I quite agree with my learned friend"—another graceful bow—"that the case he has so ably presented is so strong that it can successfully be rebutted only by an alibi so clear and so incontestable, as my learned friend has so aptly phrased it, as to convince if not satisfy . . . my bitterest enemy!" The bow, the subtle, icy intonation, edged the words. The courtroom thrilled again at the unspoken thought: *"An enemy hath done this thing!"* If, in the stillness, the prisoner had quoted the words aloud in fierce denunciation, the effect could not have been different or more startling. "And that, Your Honor, is precisely what I propose to do!"

His Honor was puzzled. He was a good judge of men; and the prisoner's face was not a bad face.

"But," he objected, "you have refused to call any witnesses for the defense. Your unsupported word will count for nothing. You cannot prove an alibi alone."

"Can't I?" said Jeff. "Watch me!"

With a single motion he was through the open

125

window. Bending branches of the nearest cottonwood broke his fall—the other trees hid his flight.

Behind him rose uproar, tumult and hullabaloo, a mass of struggling men at cross purposes. Gun in hand, the sheriff, stumbling over some one's foot—Monte's—ran to the window; but the faithful deputy was before him, blocking the way, firing with loving care—at one particular tree-trunk. He was a good shot, Jimmy. He afterward showed with pride where each ball had struck in a scant six-inch space. Vainly the sheriff tried to force his way through. There was but one stairway, and it was jammed. Before the foremost pursuer had reached the open Jeff had borrowed one of the saddled horses hitched at the rack and was away to the hills.

As Billy struggled through the press, searching for Ellinor, he found himself at Jimmy's elbow.

"A dead game sport—any turn in the road!" agreed Billy.

The deputy nodded curtly; but his answer was inconsequent:

"Rather in the brunette line—that bit of tangible evidence!"

CHAPTER XI

THE NETTLE, DANGER

"Bushel o' wheat, bushel o' rye—
All 'at ain't ready, holler 'I'!"
—Hide and Seek

DOUBLE MOUNTAIN lies lost in the desert, dwarfed by the greatness all about. Its form is that of a crater split from north to south into irregular halves. Through that narrow cleft ran a straight road, once the well-traveled thoroughfare from Rainbow to El Paso. For there was precious water within those up-heaved walls; it was but three miles from portal to portal; the slight climb to the divide had not been grudged. Time was when campfires were nightly merry to light the narrow cliffs of Double Mountain; when songs were gay to echo from them; when this had been the only watering place to break the long

127

span across the desert. The railroad had changed all this, and the silent leagues of that old road lay untrodden in the sun.

Not untrodden on this the day after Jeff had established his alibi. A traveler followed that lonely road to Double Mountain; and behind, halfway to Rainbow Range, was a streak of dust; which gained on him. The traveler's sorrel horse was weary, for it was the very horse Jeff Bransford had borrowed from the hitching-rail of the courthouse square; the traveler was that able negotiator himself; and the pursuing dust, to the best of Jeff's knowledge and belief, meant him no good tidings.

"Now, I got safe away from the foothills before day," soliloquized Jeff. "Some gentleman has overtaken me with a spyglass, I reckon. Civilization's getting this country plumb ruined! And their horses are fresh. Peg along, Alibi! Maybe I can pick up a stray horse at Double Mountain. If I can't there's no sort of use trying to get away on you! I'll play hide-and-go-seek-'em. That'll let you out, anyway, so cheer up! You done fine, old man! If I ever get out of this I'll buy you and make it all right with you. Pension you off if you think you'll like it. Get along now!"

Twenty miles to Jeff's right the railroad paralleled the wagonroad in an unbroken tangent of ninety miles' stretch. A southbound passenger train crawled along the west like a resolute centipede plodding to a date: behind the fugitive, abreast, now far ahead, creeping along the shining straightaway. Forty miles the hour

128

was her schedule; yet against this vast horizon she could hardly be said to change place until, sighting beyond her puny length, a new angle of the far western wall completed the trinomial line.

Escondido was hidden in a dip of plain—whence the name, Hidden, when done into Saxon speech. The train was lost to sight when she stopped there, but Jeff saw the tiny steam plume of her whistling rise in the clear and taintless air; long after, the faint sound of it hummed drowsily by, like passing, far-blown horns of faerie in a dream. And, at no great interval thereafter, a low-lying dust appeared suddenly on the hither rim of Escondido's sunken valley.

Jeff knew the land as you know your hallway. That line of dust marked the trail from Escondido Valley to the farther gate of Double Mountain. Even if he should be lucky enough to get a change of mounts at the spring in Double Mountain Basin he would be intercepted. Escape by flight was impossible. To fight his way out was impossible. He had no gun; and, even if he had a gun, he could not see his way to fight, under the circumstances. The men who hunted him down were only doing the right thing as they saw it. Had Jeff been guilty, it would have been a different affair. Being innocent, he could make no fight for it. He was cornered.

> "Said the little Eohippus:
> 'I'm going to be a horse!' "

So chanted Jeff, perceiving the hopelessness of his plight.

The best gift to man—or, if not the best, then at least the rarest—is the power to meet the emergency: to do your best and a little better than your best when nothing less will serve: to be a pinch hitter. It is to be thought that certain stages of affection, and more particularly the presence of its object, affect unfavorably the workings of pure intellect. Certain it is that capable Bransford, who had cut so sorry a figure in Eden garden, now, in these distressing but Eveless circumstances, rose to the occasion. Collected, resourceful, he grasped every possible angle of the situation and, with the rope virtually about his neck, cheerfully planned the impossible—the essence of his elastic plan being to climb that very rope, hand over hand, to safety.

"Going round the mountain is no good on a give-out horse. They'll follow my tracks," said Jeff to Jeff. Men who are much alone so shape their thoughts by voicing them, just as you practice conversation rather to make your own thought clear to yourself than to enlighten your victim—beg pardon—your neighbor. Just a slip of the tongue. *Vecino* is the Spanish for neighbor, you know. Not so much to enlighten your neighbor as to find out for yourself precisely what it is you think. "Hiding in the Basin is no good. Can't get out. Would I were a bird! Only one way. Got to go straight up—disappear—vanish in the air. 'Up a chimney, up——' Naw, that's backward! 'Up a chimney, down, or down a chimney, down; but not up a chimney, up, nor down a chimney, up!' So that's settled! Now let me see, says the little man. Mighty few Arcadians know me well enough not to be fooled —mebbe so. Lake? Lake won't come. He'll be busy. There's Jimmy; but Jimmy's got a shocking bad memory for faces sometimes, just now, my face. I think, maybe, I could manage Jimmy. The sheriff? That would be real awkward, I reckon. I'll just play the sheriff isn't in the bunch and build my little bluff according to that pleasing fancy; for if he comes along it is all off with little Jeff!

"Now lemme see! If Gwin's working that little old mine of his—why, he'll lie himself black in the face just for the principle of it. Mighty interestin' talker, Gwin is. And if no one's there, I'll be there. Not Jeff Bransford; he got away. I'll be Long—Tobe Long—working for Gwin. Tobe Long. I apprenticed my son to a miner, and the first thing he took was a new name!"

Far away on the side of Double Mountain he could even now see the white triangle of the tent at Gwin's mine—the Ophir—and the gray dump spilling down the hillside. There was no smoke to be seen. Jeff made up his mind there was no one at the mine—which was what he devoutly hoped—and further developed his gleeful hypothesis.

"Let's see now, Tobe. Got to study this all out. They most always leave all their kegs full of water when they go away, so they won't have to pack 'em up the first thing when they come back. If they did, I'm all right. If they didn't, I'm in a hell of a fix! They'll leave 'em full, though. Of course they did—else the kegs would all dry up and fall down." He glanced over his shoulder. "Them fellows are ten or twelve miles back, I reckon. They'll slow up so soon as they see I'm headed off. I'll have time to fix things up—if only there's water in the kegs at the mine!" He patted Alibi's head: "Now, old man, do your damnedest! It's pretty tough on you, but your part will soon be over."

Alibi had made a poor night of it, what with doubling and twisting in the foothills, the bitter water of a gyp spring, and the scanty grass of a cedar thicket; but he did his plucky best. On the legal other hand, as Jeff had prophesied, the dustmakers behind had slackened their gait when they perceived, by the dust of Escondido trail, that their allies must cut the quarry off. So Alibi held his own with the pursuit.

He came to the rising ground leading to the sheer base of Double Mountain; then to the narrow Gap where the mountain had fallen asunder in some age-old catacylsm. To the left, the dump of Ophir Mine hung on the hillside above the pass; and on the broad trail zigzagging up to it were burro-tracks, but no fresh tracks of men. The flaps of the white tent on the dump were tightly closed. There was no one at the mine. Jeff passed within the walls, through frowning gates of porphyry and gneiss, and urged Alibi up the cañon. It was half a mile to the spring. On the way he found three shaggy burros grazing beside the road. He drove them into the small pen by the spring and tossed his rope on the largest one. Then he unsaddled

Alibi, tied him to the fence by the bridle rein, and searched his pockets for an old letter. This found, he penciled a note and tied it to the saddle. It was brief:

EN ROUTE, FOUR P.M.

Please water my horse when he cools off.

Your little friend,

JEFF BRANSFORD.

P. S. Excuse haste.

He made a plain trail of high-heeled boot-tracks to the spring, where he drank deep; thence beyond, through the sandy soil, to the nearest rocky ridge. Then, careful that every step fell on a bare rock, he came circuitously back to the corral, climbed the fence, made his way to the tied burro, improvised a bridle of cunning half-hitches, slipped from the fence to the burro's back—a burro, by the way, is a donkey —named the burro anew as Balaam, and went back down the cañon at the best pace of which the be-labored and astonished Balaam was capable. As Jeff had hoped, the two other burros—or the other two burros, to be precise—followed sociably, braying remonstrance.

Without the mouth of the cañon Jeff rode up the steep trail to the mine, also to the great disgust of his mount; but he must not walk—it would leave boot-tracks. For the same reason, after freeing Balaam, his first action was to pull off the telltale boots and replace them with the smallest pair of hobnailed miner's shoes in the tent. With these he carefully obliterated the few boot-tracks at the tent door.

133

The water-kegs were full; Jeff swore his joyful gratitude and turned his eye to the plain. The pursuing dust was still far away—seven miles, he estimated, or possibly eight. The three burros nibbled on the bushes below the dump; plainly intending to stay round camp with an eye for possible tips. Jeff gave his whole-hearted attention to the *mise-en-scène*.

Never did stage manager toil so hard, so faithfully, so effectively as this one—or with so great a need. He took stock of the available stage properties, beginning with a careful inventory of the grub-chest. To betray ignorance of its possibilities or deficiencies would be fatal. Following a narrow trail round a little shoulder of hill, he found the powder magazine. Taking three sticks of dynamite, with fuse and caps, he searched the tent for the candle-box, lit a candle and went into the tunnel with a brisk trot. "If this was a case of fight, now, I'd have some pretty fair weapons here for close quarters," said Jeff; "but the way I'm fixed I can't. No fighting goes—unless Lake comes."

In the tunnel his luck held good. He found a number of good-sized chunks of rock stacked along the wall near the breast—evidently reserved for the ore pile at a more convenient season. Beneath three of the largest of these rocks he carefully adjusted the three sticks of giant powder, properly capped and fused, lit the fuses and retreated to the safety of the dump. Three muffled detonations followed at short intervals. Having thus announced the presence of mining operations, he built a fire on the kitchen side of the dump to further adver-

134

tise a mind conscious of its own rectitude. The pleasant shadow of the hills was cool about him; the flame rose clear and bright in the windless air, to be seen from far away.

He looked at the location papers in the monument by the ore stack; simultaneously, by way of economizing time, emptying a can of salmon. This was partly for the added verisimilitude of the empty tin, partly because he was ravenously hungry. You may guess how he emptied the tin.

The mine had changed owners since Jeff's knowledge of it. It was no longer Gwin's sole property. The notice bore the signatures of J. Gwin, C. W. Sanders and Walter Fleck. Jeff grinned and his eye brightened. He knew Fleck only slightly; but Fleck's reputation among the cowmen was good—that is to say, as you would see it, very bad.

Pappy Sanders, postmaster and storekeeper of Escondido, was an old and sorely tried friend of Jeff's. If Pappy had grub-staked the outfit—— A far-away plan began to shape vaguely in his fertile brain. He took the little turquoise horse from his pocket and laid it in the till of the violated trunk. Were you told about the violated trunk? Never mind—he had done any amount of other things of which you have not been told; for it was his task, in the brief time allotted to him, to master all the innumerable details needful for an intelligent reading of his part. He must make no blunders.

He toiled like two men, each swifter and more

savagely efficient than himself; he upset the prim, old he-maidenish order of that carefully packed, spick-and-span camp; he rumpled the beds; strewed old clothes, books, candles, specimens, pipes and cigarette papers with lavish hand; made untidy, sprawling heaps of tin plates; knives, forks and spoons; spilled candle-grease and tobacco on the scoured table; and generally gave things a cozy and habitable appearance.

He gave a hundred deft touches here and there. He spread an open book face downward on the table. (It was "Alice in Wonderland," and he opened it at the Mock-Turtle.) Meanwhile an unoccupied eye snatched titles from a shelf of books against possible question; he penned a short note to himself—Mr. Tobe Long—in Gwin's handwriting, folded the note to creases, twisted it to a spill, lit it, burned a corner of it, pinched it out and threw it under the table; and, while doing these and other things, he somehow managed to shed every article of Jeff Bransford's clothing and to put on the work-stained garments of a miner.

The perspiration on his face was no stage make-up, but good, honest sweat. He rubbed stone-dust and sand on his sweaty arms and into his sweaty hair; he rubbed most of it from his hair and into the two-days' stubble on his face, simultaneously fishing razor and mug from the trunk, leaving them in evidence on the table. He worked stone-dust into his ears, behind his ears; he grimed it on forehead and neck; he even dropped a little into his shoes, which all this while had been performing independent miracles to make the camp look comfortable. He threw on a dingy cap, thrust in the cap a miner's candlestick, with a lighted candle, that it might properly drip upon him while he arranged further details—and so faced the world as Tobe Long, a stooped and overworked man!

Mr. Tobe Long, working with feverish haste, dug a small cave halfway down the steep side of the dump farthest from the road and buried therein a tightly rolled bundle containing every article appertaining to the defunct Bransford, with the single exception of the little eohippus; a pocketknife, which a miner must have to cut powder and fuse, having been found in the trunk—what time also the little turquoise horse was transferred to Mr. Long's pocket to bring him luck in his new career—a poor thing compared with the cowman's keen blade, but better for Mr. Long's purposes, as smelling strongly of dynamite. Then Mr. Long—Tobe—hid the grave by sliding and shoveling broken rock down the dump upon it.

Next he threw into a wheelbarrow drills, spoon, tamping stick, gads, drill-hammer, rock-hammer, canteen, shovel and pick—taking care, even in his haste, to select a properly matched set of drills—and trundled the barrow up the drift at a pace which would give a Miners' Union the rabies. At the breast, he unshipped his cargo in right miner's fashion, the drills in a graduated stepladder row along the wall; loaded the barrow with broken ore, a bit of charred fuse showing at the top, and wheeled it out at the same unprofessional gait, leaving it on the dump just above the spot where his late sepulchral rites had freshened the appearance of the sunbeaten dump.

He next performed his ablutions in an amateurish and perfunctory fashion, scrupulously observing a well-defined waterline.

"There!" said Mr. Long. "I near made a break that time!" He went back to the barrow and trundled it assiduously to the tunnel's mouth and back several times, carefully never in quite the same place—finally leaving it not above the sepulchered spoil, but near the ore stack, as befitted its valuable contents. "I got to think of everything. One wrong break'll fix me good!" said Mr. Long. He felt his neck delicately, as if he detected some foreign presence there. "In the tunnel, now, there's only the one place where the wheel can go; so it don't matter so much in there."

The fire having now burned down to proper coals, Mr. Long set about supper; with the corner of his eye on the lookout for the pursuers of the late Bransford. He set the coffee-pot by the fire—they were now in the edge of the tarbrush; there were only two of them. He put on a pot of potatoes in their jackets—he could see them plainly, diminutive black horsemen twinkling through the brush; he sliced bacon into a frying-pan and put it aside to await his cue; he disposed other cooking ware in lifelike attitudes near the fire—they were in the long shadow of Double Mountain; their horses were jaded; they rode slowly. He dropped the sour-dough jar and placed the broken pieces where they would be inconspicuously visible. Having thus a perfectly obvious excuse for not having sour-dough bread, which requires thirty-six hours of running start for preliminary rising, Jeff—Mr. Tobe Long—mixed up a just-as-good baking-powder substitute—they rode like young men; they rode like young men not to the saddle born, and Tobe permitted himself a chuckle: "By hooky, I've got an even chance for my little bluff!"

He shook his head reprovingly at himself for this last admission. With every minute he looked more like Tobe Long than ever—if only there had been any Tobe Long to look like. His mind ran upon nuggets, pockets, placers, faults, true fissure veins, the cyanide process, concentrates, chlorides, sulphides, assays, leases and bonds; his face took on the strained wistfulness which marks the confirmed prospector: he *was* Tobe Long!

The bell rang.

CHAPTER XII

THE SIEGE OF DOUBLE MOUNTAIN

"Timeo Danaos et dona ferentes."
—The Dictionary

"Ho-o-e-ee! Hello-o!"

As the curtain rose to the flying echoes Long stepped to the edge of the dump, frying-pan in hand, and sent back an answering shout in the startled high note of a lonely man taken unawares.

"Hello-o!" He brandished his hospitable pan. Then he put it down, cupped hands to mouth and trumpeted a hearty welcome: "Chuck! Come up! Supper's ready!"

"Can't! See any one go by about two hours ago?"

"Hey? Louder!"

"See a man on a sorrel horse?"

"No-o! I been in the tunnel. Come up!"

"Can't. We're after an outlaw!"

"What?"

"After a murderer!"

"Wait a minute! I'll be down. Too hard to yell so far."

Mr. Long started precipitately down the zigzag; but the riders had got all the information of interest that Mr. Long could furnish and they were eager to be in at the death.

"Can't wait! He's inside the mountain, somewheres. Some of the boys are waiting for him at the other end." They rode on.

Mr. Long posed for a statue of Disappointment, hung on the steep trail rather as if he might conclude to coil himself into a ball and roll down the hill to overtake them.

"Stop as you come back!" he bellowed. "Want to hear about it."

Did Jeff—Mr. Long—did Mr. Long now attempt to escape? Not so. Gifted with prevision beyond most, Mr. Long's mind misgave him that these young men would be baffled in their pleasing expectations. They would be back before sundown, very cross; and a miner's brogan leaves a track not to be missed.

That Mr. Long was unfeignedly fatigued from the varied efforts of the day need not be mentioned, for that alone would not have stayed his flight; but the nearest water, save Escondido, was thirty-five miles; and at Escondido he would be watched for—not to say that, when he was missed, some of the searching party would straightway go to Escondido to frustrate him. Present escape was not to be thought of.

Instead, Mr. Long made a hearty meal from the simple viands that had been in course of preparation when he was surprised, eked out by canned corn fried in bacon grease to a crisp, golden brown. Then, after a cigarette, he betook himself to sharpening tools with laudable industry. The tools were already sharp, but that did not stop Mr. Long. He built a fire in the forge, set up a stepladder of matched drills in the blackened water of the tempering tub; he thrust a gad and one short drill into the fire. When the gad was at a good cherry heat he thrust it hissing into the tub to bring the water to a convincing temperature; and when reheated he did it again. From time to time he held the one drill to the anvil and shaped it, drawing it alternately to a chisel bit or a bull bit. Mr. Long could sharpen a drill with any, having been, in very truth, a miner of sorts—he could toy thus with one drill without giving it any very careful attention, and his thoughts were now busy on how best to be Mr. Long.

Accordingly from time to time he added an artistic touch to Mr. Long—grime under his fingernails, a smudge of smut on an eyebrow. His hands displeased him. After some experimenting to get the proper heat of it he grasped the partially cooled gad with the drill-pincers and held it very lightly to a favored few of those portions of the hand known to chiromaniacs as the mounts of Jupiter, Saturn and other extinct immortals.

142

Satisfactory blisters-while-you-wait were thus obtained. These were pricked with a pin; some were torn to tatters, with dust and coal rubbed in to give them a venerable appearance. The pain was no light matter; but Mr. Long had a real affection for Mr. Bransford's neck, and it is trifles like these that make perfection.

The next expedient was even more heroic. Mr. Long assiduously put stone-dust in one eye, leaving it tearful, bloodshot and violently inflamed; and the other one was sympathetically red. "Bit o' steel in my eye," explained Mr. Long. Unselfish devotion such as this is all too rare.

All this while, at proper intervals, Mr. Long sharpened and resharpened that one long-suffering drill. He tripped into the tunnel and smote a mighty blow upon the country rock with a pick—therefore qualifying that pick for repointing—and laid it on the forge as next on the list.

What further outrage he meditated is not known, for he now heard a horse coming up the trail. He was beating out a merry tattoo when a white-hatted head rose through a trapdoor—rose above the level of the dump, rather.

Hammer in hand, Long straightened up joyfully as best he could, but could not straighten up the telltale droop of his shoulders. It was not altogether assumed, either, this hump. Jeff—Mr. Long—had not done so much work of this sort for years and there was a very real pain between his shoulderblades. Still, but for the exigencies of art, he might have borne his neck less turtlewise than he did.

"Hello! Get him? Where's your pardner?"

"Watching the gap." The young man, rather breathless from the climb, answered the last question first as he led his horse on the dump. "No, we didn't get him; but he can't get away. Hiding somewhere in the Basin afoot. Found his horse. Pretty well done up." The insolence of the outlaw's letter smote him afresh; he reddened. "No tracks going out of the Basin. Two of our friends guarding the other end. They say he can't get out over the cliffs anywhere. That so?" The speech came jerkily; he was still short of breath from his scramble.

"Not without a flying machine," said Long. "No way out that I know of, except where the wagonroad goes. What's he done?"

"Robbery! Murder! We'll see that he don't get out by the wagonroad," asserted the youth confidently. "Watch the gaps and starve him out!"

"Oh, speaking of starving," said Tobe, "go into the tent and I'll bring you some supper while you tell me about it. Baked up another batch of bread on the chance you'd come back."

"Why, thank you very much, Mr.——"

"Long—Tobe Long."

"Mr. Long. My name is Gurdon Steele. Glad to meet you. Why, if you will be so kind—that is what I came up to see you about. If you can let us have what we need of course we will pay you for it."

"Of course you won't!" It had not needed the offer to place Mr. Gurdon Steele quite accurately. He was a handsome lad, fresh-complexioned, dressed in the Western manner as practised on the Boardwalk. "You're welcome to what I got, sure; but I ain't got much variety. Gwin, the old liar, said he was coming out the twentieth—and sure enough he didn't; so the grub's running low. Table in the tent—come on!"

"Oh, no, I couldn't, you know! Rex—that's my partner—is quite as hungry as I am, you see; but if you could give me something—anything you have— to take down there? I really couldn't, you know!" The admirable doctrine of *noblesse oblige* in its delicate application by this politeness, was easier for its practitioner than to put it into words suited to the comprehension of his hearer; he concluded lamely: "I'll take it down there and we will eat it together."

"See here," said Tobe, "I'm as hungry to hear about your outlaw as you are to eat. I'll just throw my bedding and a lot of chuck on your saddle. We'll carry the coffee-pot and frying-pan in our hands—and the sugar-can and things like that. You can tank up and give me the news in small chunks at the same time. Afterward two of us can sleep while one stands guard."

This was done. It was growing dark when they reached the bottom of the hill. The third guardsman had built a fire.

"Rex, this is Mr. Long, who has been kind enough to grubstake us and share our watch with us."

145

Mr. Steele, you have observed, had accepted Mr. Long without question; but his first impression of Mr. Long had been gained under circumstances highly favorable to the designs of the latter gentleman. Mr. Steele had come upon him unexpectedly, finding him as it were *in medias res*, with all his skillfully arranged scenery to aid the illusion. The case was now otherwise—the thousand-tongued vouching of his background lacked to him; Mr. Long had naught save his own unthinkable audacity to belie his face withal. From the first instant Mr. Rex Griffith was the prey of suspicions—acute, bigoted, churlish, deep, dark, distrustful, damnable, and so on down to zealous. He had a sharp eye; he wore no puttees; and Mr. Long had a vaguely uncomfortable memory, holding over from some previous incarnation, of having seen that long, shrewd face in a courtroom.

The host, on hospitable rites intent, likewise all ears and eager questionings, was all unconscious of hostile surveillance. Nothing could be more carefree, more at ease than his bearing; his pleasant anticipatory excitement was the natural outlook for a lonely and newsless man. As the hart panteth for the water, so he thirsted for the story; but his impatient, hasty questions, following false scents, delayed the telling of the Arcadian tale. So innocent was he, so open and aboveboard, that Griffith, watching, alert, felt thoroughly ashamed of himself. Yet he watched, doubting still, though his reason rebelled at the monstrous imaginings of his heart. That the outlaw, unarmed and

146

unasked, should venture—Pshaw! Such effrontery was inconceivable. He allowed Steele to tell the story, himself contributing only an occasional crafty question designed to enable his host to betray himself.

"Bransford?" interrupted Mr. Long. "Not Jeff Bransford—up South Rainbow way?"

"That's the man," said Steele.

"I don't believe it," said Long flatly. He was sipping coffee with his guests; he put his cup down. "I know him, a little. He don't——"

"Oh, there's no doubt of it!" interrupted Steele in his turn. He detailed the circumstances with skilful care. "Besides, why did he run away? Gee! You ought to have seen that escape! It was splendid!"

"Well, now, who'd 'a' thought that?" demanded Long, still only half convinced. "He didn't strike me like that kind of a man. Well, you never can tell! How come you fellows to be chasin' him?"

"You see," said Steele, "every one was sure he had gone up to Rainbow. The sheriff and posse is up there now, looking for him; but we four—Stone and Harlow, the chaps at the other end, were with us, you know—we were up in the foothills on a deerhunt. We were out early—sun-up is the best time for deer, they tell me—and we had a spyglass. Well, we just happened to see a man ride out from between two hills, quite a way off. Stone noticed right away that he was riding a sorrel horse. It was a sorrel horse that Bransford stole, you know. We didn't suspect, though, who it was till a bit later. Then Rex tried to pick him up

147

again and saw that he was going out of his way to avoid the ridges—keeping cover, you know. Then we caught on and took after him pell-mell. He had a big start; but he was riding slowly so as not to make a dust—that is, till he saw our dust. Then he lit out."

"You're not deputies, then?" said Long.

"Oh, no, not at all!" said Steele, secretly flattered. "So Harlow and Stone galloped off to town. The program was that they'd wire down to Escondido to have horses ready for them, come down on Number Six and head him off. They were not to tell any one in Arcadia. There's five thousand dollars' reward out for him—but it isn't that exactly. It was a cowardly, beastly murder, don't you know; and we thought it would be rather a big thing if we could take him alone."

"You got him penned all right," said Tobe. "He can't get out, so far as I know, unless he runs over us or the men at the other end. By George, we must get away from this fire, too!" He set the example, dragging the bedding with him to the shelter of a big rock. "He could pick us off too slick here in the light. How're you going to get him? There's a heap of country in that Basin, all rough and broken, full o' boulders—mighty good cover."

"Starve him out!" said Griffith. This was base deceit. Deep in his heart he believed that the quarry sat beside him, well fed and contented. Yet the unthinkable insolence of it—if this were indeed Bransford—dulled his belief.

Long laughed as he spread down the bed. "He'll shoot a deer. Maybe, if he had it all planned out, he may have grub cached in there somewhere. There's watertanks in the rocks. Say, what are your pardners at the other side going to do for grub?"

"Oh, they brought out cheese and crackers and stuff," said Gurd.

"I'll tell you what, boys, you've bit off more than you can chaw," said Jeff—Tobe, that is. "He can't get out without a fight—but, then, you can't go in there to hunt for him without weakening your guard; and he'd be under shelter and have all the best of it. He'd shoot you so dead you'd never know what happened. I don't want none of it! I'd as lief put on boxing gloves and crawl into a hole after a bear! Look here, now, this is your show; but I'm a heap older'n you boys. Want to know what I think?"

"Certainly," said Rex.

"Goin' to talk turkey to me?" An avaricious light came into Long's eyes.

"Of course; you're in on the reward," said Rex diffidently and rather stiffly. "We are not in this for the money."

"I can use the money—whatever share you want to give me," said Long dryly; "but if you take my advice my share won't be but a little. I think you ought to keep under shelter at the mouth of this cañon—one of you—and let the other one go to Escondido and send for help, quick, and a lot of it."

"What's the matter with you going?" asked Griffith

disingenuously. He wanted Long to show his hand. It would never do to abandon the siege of Double Mountain to arrest this *soidisant* Long on mere suspicion. On the other hand, Mr. Rex Griffith had no idea of letting Long escape his clutches until his identity was established, one way or the other, beyond all question.

That was why Long declined the offer. His honest gaze shifted. "I ain't much of a rider," he said evasively. Young Griffith read correctly the thought which the excuse concealed. Evidently Long considered himself an elder soldier, if not a better, than either of his two young guests, but wished to spare their feelings by not letting them find it out. Griffith found this plain solution inconsistent with his homicidal theory: a murderer, fleeing for his life, would have jumped at the chance.

There are two sides to every question. Let us, this once, prove both sides. Wholly oblivious to Griffith's lynx-eyed watchfulness and his leading questions, Mr. Long yet recognized the futility of an attempt to ride away on Mr. Griffith's horse with Mr. Griffith's benison. There we have the other point of view.

"We'll have to send for grub anyway," pursued the sagacious Mr. Long. "I've only got a little left; and that old liar, Gwin, won't be out for four days—if he comes then. And—er—look here now—if I was you boys I'd let the sheriff and his posse smoke your badger out. They get paid to tend to that—and it looks to me like some one was going to get hurt. You've done enough."

150

All this advice was so palpably sound that the doubter was, for the second, staggered—for a second only. This was the man he had seen in the prisoner's dock. He was morally sure of it. For all the difference of appearance, this was the man. Yet those blasts— the far-seen fire—the hearty welcome—this delivery of himself into their hands? . . . Griffith scarcely knew what he did think. He blamed himself for his un- worthy suspicions; he blamed Gurdy more for having no suspicions at all.

"Anything else?" he said. "That sounds good."

Tobe studied for some time.

"Well," he said at last, "there may be some way he can get out. I don't think he can—but he might find a way. He knows he's trapped; but likely he has no idea yet how many of us there are. So we know he'll try, and he won't be just climbing for fun. He'll take a chance."

Steele broke in:

"He didn't leave any rope on his saddle."

Tobe nodded.

"So he means to try it. Now here's five of us here. It seems to me that some one ought to ride round the mountain the first thing in the morning, and every day afterward—only here's hoping there won't be many of 'em—to look for tracks. There isn't one chance in a hundred he can climb out; but if he goes out of here afoot we've got him sure. The man on guard wants to keep in shelter. It's light to-night—there's no chance for him to slip out without being seen. You say the old watchman ain't dead yet, Mr. Griffith?"

"No. The latest bulletin was that he was almost holding his own."

"Hope he gets well," said Long. "Good old geezer! Now, cap, I've worked hard and you've ridden hard. Better set your guards and let the other two take a little snooze."

Griffith was not proof against the insidious flattery of this unhesitant preference. He flushed with embarrassment and pleasure.

"Well, if I'm to be captain, Gurd will take the first guard—till eleven. Then you come on till two, Mr. Long. I'll stand from then on till daylight."

In five minutes Mr. Long was enjoying the calm and restful sleep of fatigued innocence; but his poor captain was doomed to have a bad night of it, with two Bransfords on his hands—one in the Basin and one in the bed beside him. His head was dizzy with the vicious circle. Like the gentlewoman of the nursery rhyme, he was tempted to cry: "Lawk 'a' mercy on me, this is none of I!"

If he haled his bedmate to justice and the real Bransford got away—that would be a nice predicament for an ambitious young man! He was sensitive to ridicule, and he saw here such an opportunity to earn it as knocks but once at any man's door.

If, on the other hand, while he held Bransford cooped tightly in the Basin, this thrice-accursed Long should escape him and there should be no Bransford

in the Basin—— What nonsense! What utter twad-
dle! Bransford was in the Basin. He had found his
horse and saddle, his tracks; no tracks had come out
of the Basin. Immediately on the discovery of the outlaw's horse, Gurd had ridden back posthaste and held
the pass while he, the captain, had gone to the mouth
of the southern cañon and posted his friends. He had
watched for tracks of a footman every step of the way,
going and coming; there had been no tracks. Bransford was in the Basin. He watched the face of the
sleeping man. But, by Heaven, this was Bransford!

Was ever a poor captain in such a predicament? A
moment before he had fully and definitely decided
once for all that this man was not Bransford, could
not be Bransford; that it was not possible! His reason
unwaveringly told him one thing, his eyesight the
other! . . . Yet Bransford, or an unfortunate twin of
his, lay now beside him—and, for further mockery,
slept peacefully, serene, untroubled. . . . He looked
upon the elusive Mr. Long with a species of horror!
The face was drawn and lined. Yet, but forty-eight
hours of tension would have left Bransford's face not
otherwise. He had noticed Bransford's hands in the
courtroom—noticed their well-kept whiteness, due, as
he had decided, to the perennial cowboy glove. This
man's hands, as he had seen by the campfire, were
blistered and calloused! Callouses were not made in
a day. He took another look at Long. Oh, thunder!

He crept from bed. He whispered a word to sentry
Steele; not to outline the distressing state of his own

153

mind, but merely to request Steele not to shoot him, as he was going up to the mine.

He climbed up the trail, chewing the unpalatable thought that Gurdon had seen nothing amiss—yet Gurd had been at the trial! The captain began to wish he had never gone on that deerhunt.

He went into the tent, struck a match, lit a candle and examined everything closely. There was no gun in the camp and no cartridges. He found the spill of twisted paper under the table, smothered his qualms and read it. He noted the open book for future examination in English. And now Tobe's labors had their late reward, for Rex missed nothing. Every effort brought fresh disappointment and every disappointment spurred him to fresh effort. He went into the tunnel; he scrutinized everything, even to the drills in the tub. The food supply tallied with Long's account. No detail escaped him and every detail confirmed the growing belief that he, Captain Griffith, was a doddering imbecile.

He returned to the outpost, convinced at last. Nevertheless, merely to quiet the ravings of his insubordinate instincts, now in open revolt, he restaked the horses nearer to camp and cautiously carried both saddles to the head of the bed. Concession merely encouraged the rebels to further and successful outrages —the government was overthrown.

He drew sentry Steele aside and imparted his doubts. That faithful follower heaped scorn, mockery, laughter and abuse upon his shrinking superior: re-

counted all the points, from the first blasts of dynamite to the present moment, which favored the chari-
table belief above mentioned as newly entertained by
Captain Griffith concerning himself. This belief of
Captain Griffith was amply indorsed by his sub-
ordinate in terms of point and versatility.

"Of course they look alike. I noticed that the minute
I saw him—the same amount of legs and arms, fea-
tures all in the fore part of his head, hair on top, one
body—wonderful! Why, you pitiful ass, that Bransford person was a mighty keen-looking man in any
company. This fellow's a yokel—an old, rusty, cap-
and-ball, single-shot muzzle-loader. The Bransford
was an automatic, steel-frame, high velocity——"

"The better head he has the more apt he is to do
the unexpected——"

"Aw, shut up! You've got incipient paresis! Stuff
your ears in your mouth and go to sleep!"

The captain sought his couch convinced, but holding his first opinion, savagely minded to arrest Mr.
Long rather than let him have a gun to stand guard
with. He was spared the decision. Mr. Long declined
Gurdon's proffered gun, saying that he would be right
there and he was a poor shot anyway.

Gurdon slept; Long took his place—and Captain
Rex, from the bed, watched the watcher. Never was
there a more faithful sentinel than Mr. Long. Without relaxing his vigilance even to smoke, he strained
every faculty lest the wily Bransford should creep out
through the shadows. The captain saw him, a stooped

155

figure, sitting motionless by his rock, always alert, peering this way and that, turning his head to listen. Once Tobe saw something. He crept noiselessly to the bed and shook his chief. Griffith came, with his gun. Something was stirring in the bushes. After a little it moved out of the shadows. It was a prowling coyote. The captain went back to bed once more convinced of Long's fidelity, but resolved to keep a relentless eye on him just the same. And all unawares, as he revolved the day's events in his mind, the captain dropped off to troubled sleep.

Mr. Long woke him at three. There had been a temptation to ride away, but the saddles were at the head of the bed, the ground was stony; he would be heard. He might have made an attempt to get both guns from under the pillow, but detection meant ruin for him, since to shoot these boys or to hurt them was out of the question. Escape by violence would have been easy and assured. Jeff preferred to trust his wits. He was enjoying himself very much.

When the captain got his relentless eyes open and realized what had chanced he saw that further doubt was unworthy. Half an hour later the unworthy captain stole noiselessly to Long's bedside and saw, to his utter rage and distraction, that Mr. Bransford was there again. It was almost too much to bear. He felt that he should always hate Long, even after Bransford was safely hanged. Bransford's head had slipped from Long's pillow. Hating himself, Griffith subtly withdrew the miner's folded overalls and went through the pockets.

He found there a knife smelling of dynamite, matches, a turquoise carved to what was plainly meant to be the form of a bad-tempered horse, and two small specimens of ore!

Altogether, the captain passed a wild and whirling night.

CHAPTER XIII

THE SIEGE OF DOUBLE MOUNTAIN
(*Continued*)

"If the bowl had been stronger
My tale had been longer."
—Mother Goose

WHEN the sun peeped over Rainbow Range, Captain Griffith bent over Tobe Long's bed. His eyes were aching, burned and sunken; the lids twitched; his face was haggard and drawn—but he had arrived at an unalterable decision. This thing could not and should not go on. His brain reeled now—another such night would entitle him to state protection.

He shook Mr. Long roughly.

"See here! I believe you're Bransford himself!"

Thus taken off his guard, Long threw back the bedding, rose to one elbow, still half asleep, and reached for his shoes, laughing and yawning alternately. Then, as he woke up a little more, he saw a better way to

dress, dropped the shoes and unfurled his pillow—
which, by day, he wore as overalls. Fumbling behind
him, where the pillow had lain, he found a much-
soiled handkerchief and tenderly dabbed at his
swollen eye.

"Bit of steel in my eye from a drill-head," he explained. "Jiminy, but it's sore!"

Plainly he took the accusation as a pleasantry calling for no answer.

"I mean it! I'm going to keep you under guard!"
said Captain Griffith bitingly.

Poor, sleepy Tobe, halfway into his overalls, stared
up at Mr. Griffith; his mouth dropped open—he was
quite at a loss for words. The captain glared back at
him. Tobe kicked the overalls off and cuddled back
into bed.

"Bully!" he said. "Then I won't have to get breakfast!"

Gurdon Steele sat up in bed, a happy man. His eye
gave Mr. Long a discreetly confidential look, as of one
who restrains himself, out of instinctive politeness,
from a sympathetic and meaningful tap of one's forehead. A new thought struck Mr. Long. He reached
over behind Steele for the rifle at the bed's edge and
thrust it into the latter's hands.

"Here, Boy Scout! Watch me!" he whispered.
"Don't let me escape while I sleep a few lines! I'm
Bransford!"

Gurdie rubbed his eyes and giggled.

"Don't you mind Rex. That's the worst of this pipe

159

habit. You never can tell how they'll break out next."

"Yes, laugh, you blind bat!" said Rex bitterly. "I've got him all the same, and I'm going to keep him while you go to Escondido!" His rifle was tucked under his arm; he patted the barrel significantly.

It slowly dawned upon Mr. Long that Captain Griffith was not joking, after all, and an angry man was he. He sat up in bed.

"Oh, piffle! Oh, fudge! Oh, pickled moonshine! If I'm Bransford what the deuce am I doing here? Why, you was both asleep! I could 'a' shot your silly heads off and you'd 'a' never woke up. You make me tired!"

"Don't mind him, Long. He'll feel better when he takes a nap," said Gurd joyfully. "He has poor spells like this and he misses his nurse. We always make allowances for him."

Mr. Long's indignation at last overcame his politeness, and in his wrath he attacked friend and foe indiscriminately.

"Do you mean to tell me you two puling infants are out hunting down a man you never saw? Don't the men at the other side know him either? By jinks, you hike out o' this after breakfast and send for some grown-up men. I want part of that reward—and I'm going to have it! Look here!" He turned blackly to Gurdon. "Are you sure that Bransford, or any one else, came in here at all yesterday, or did you dream it? Or was it all a damfool kid joke? Listen here! I worked like a dog yesterday. If you had me stand guard three hours, tired as I was, for nothing, there's

160

going to be more to it. What kind of a sack-and-snipe trick is this, anyway? You just come one at a time and I'll lick the stuffin' out o' both o' you! I ain't feelin' like any schoolboy pranks just now."

"No, no; that part's all straight. Bransford's in there, all right," protested Gurdon. "If you hadn't been working in the tunnel you'd have seen him when he went by. Here's the note he left. And his horse and saddle are up at the spring. We left the horse there because he was lame and about all in. Bransford can't get away on him. Rex is just excited—that's all the matter with him. Hankering for glory! I told him last night not to make a driveling idiot of himself. Here, read this insolent note, will you?"

Long glowered at the note and flung it aside. "Anybody could 'a' wrote that! How am I to know this thing ain't some more of your funny streaks? You take these horses to water and bring back Bransford's horse and saddle, and then I'll know what to believe. Be damn sure you bring them, too, or we'll go to producing glory right here—great gobs and chunks of it! You Griffith! put down that gun or I'll knock your fool head off! I'm takin' charge of this outfit now, and don't you forget it! And I don't want no maniac wanderin' round me with a gun. You go to gatherin' up wood as fast as ever God'll let you!"

"Say, I was mistaken," said the deposed leader, thoroughly convinced once more. "You do look like Bransford, you know." He laid down his rifle obediently.

161

"Look like your grandmother's left hind foot!" sneered the outraged miner. "My eyes is brown and so's Bransford's. Outside o' that——"

"No, but you do, a little," said his ally, Steele. "I noticed it myself, last night. Not much—but still there's a resemblance. Poor Cap Griffith just let his nerves and imagination run away with him—that's all."

Long sniffed. "Funny I never heard of it before," he said. He was somewhat mollified, nevertheless; and, while cooking breakfast, he received very graciously a stammered and half-hearted apology from young Mr. Griffith, now reduced to the ranks. "Oh, that's all right, kid. But say—you be careful and don't shoot your pardner when he comes back."

Gurdon brought back the sorrel horse and the saddle, thereby allaying Mr. Long's wrathful mistrust that the whole affair was a practical joke.

"I told you butter wouldn't suit the works!" said Rex triumphantly, and watched the working of his test with a jealous eye.

Long knew his Alice. " 'But it was the best butter,' " he said. He surveyed the sorrel horse; his eye brightened. "We'll whack up that blood-money yet," he announced confidently. "Now I'm going to walk over to the south side and get one of those fellows to ride sign round the mountain. You boys can sleep, turn and turn about, till I get back. Then I want Steele to go to Escondido and wire up to Arcadia that we've got our bear by the tail and want help to turn him loose,

162

and tell Pappy Sanders to send me out some grub or I'll skin him. Pappy's putting up for the mine, you know. I'll stay here and keep an eye on Griffith." He gave that luckless warrior a jeering look, as one who has forgiven but not forgotten.

"Why don't you ride one of our horses?" said Gurdon.

"Want to keep 'em fresh. Then if Bransford gets out over the cliffs you can run him down like a mad dog," said Tobe. "Besides, if I ride a fresh horse in here he'll maybe shoot me to get the horse; and if he could catch you lads away from shelter maybe so he'd make a dash for it, a-shootin'. See here! If I was dodgin' in here like him—know what I'd do? I'd just shoot a few lines on general principles to draw you away from the gates. Then if you went in to see about it I'd either kill you if I had to, or slip out if you give me the chance. You just stay right here, whatever happens. Keep under shelter and keep your horses right by you. We got him bottled up and we won't draw the cork till the sheriff comes. I'll tell 'em to do the same way at the other end. I won't take any gun with me and I'll stick to the big main road. That way Bransford won't feel no call to shoot me. Likely he's 'way up in the cliffs, anyhow."

"Ride the sorrel horse then, why don't you? He isn't lame enough to hurt much, but he's lame enough that Bransford won't want him." Thus Mr. Griffith, again dissimulating. Every detail of Mr. Long's plan forestalled suspicion. That these measures were precisely calculated to disarm suspicion now occurred to Griffith's stubborn mind. For he had a stubborn mind; the morning's coffee had cleared it of cobwebs, and it clung more tenaciously than ever to the untenable and thrice-exploded theory that Long and Bransford were one and inseparable, now and forever.

He meditated an ungenerous scheme for vindication and, to that end, wished Mr. Long to ride the sorrel horse. For Mr. Long, if he were indeed the murderer —as, of course, he was—would indubitably, upon some plausible pretext, attempt to pass the guards at the farther end of the trip, where was no clear-eyed Griffith on guard. What more plausible that a modification of the plan already rehearsed—for Long to tell the wardens that Griffith had sent him to telegraph to the sheriff? Let him once pass those warders on any pretext! That would be final betrayal, for all his shrewdness. There was no possibility that Long and Bransford could complete their escape on that lame sorrel. He would not be allowed to get much of a start —just enough to betray himself. Then he, Griffith, would bring them back in triumph.

It was a good scheme: all things considered, it reflected great credit upon Mr. Griffith's imagination. As in Poe's game of "odd or even," where you must outguess your opponent and follow his thought, Mr. Rex Griffith had guessed correctly in every respect. Such, indeed, had been Mr. Long's plan. Only Rex did not guess quite often enough. Mr. Long had guessed just one layer deeper—namely, that Mr. Griffith

164

would follow his thought correctly and also follow him. Therefore Mr. Long switched again. It was a bully game—better than poker. Mr. Long enjoyed it very much.

Just as Rex expected, Tobe allowed himself to be overpersuaded and rode the sorrel horse. He renamed the sorrel horse Goldie, on the spot, saddled him awkwardly, mounted in like manner, and rode into the shadowy depths of Double Mountain.

Once he was out of sight Mr. Griffith followed, despite the angry protest of Mr. Steele—alleging falsely that he was going to try for a deer.

Tobe rode slowly up the crooked and brush-lined cañon. Behind him, cautiously hidden, came Griffith, the hawk-eyed avenger—waiting at each bend until Mr. Long had passed the next one, for closer observation of how Mr. Long bore himself in solitude.

Mr. Long bore himself most disappointingly. He rode slowly and awkwardly, scanning with anxious care the hillsides before him. Not once did he look back lest he should detect Mr. Griffith. Near the summit the Goldie horse shied and jumped. It was only one little jump, whereunto Goldie had been privately instigated by Mr. Long's thumb—"thumbing" a horse, as done by one conversant with equine anatomy, produces surprising results!—but it caught Mr. Long unawares and tumbled him ignominiously in the dust.

Mr. Long sat in the sand and rubbed his shoulder: Goldie turned and looked down at him in unqualified astonishment. Mr. Long then cursed Mr. Bransford's sorrel horse; he cursed Mr. Bransford for bringing the sorrel horse; he cursed himself for riding the sorrel horse; he cursed Mr. Griffith, with one last, longest, heart-felt, crackling, hair-raising, comprehensive and masterly curse, for having persuaded him to ride the sorrel horse. Then he tied the sorrel horse to a bush and hobbled on afoot, saying it all over backward.

Poor Griffith experienced the most intense mortification—except one—of his life. This was conclusive. Bransford was reputed the best rider in Rainbow. This was Long. He was convinced, positively, finally and irrevocably. He did not even follow Mr. Long to the other side of Double Mountain, but turned back to camp, keeping a sharp eye out for traces of the real Bransford; to no effect. It was only by chance—a real chance—that, clambering on the gatepost cliffs to examine a curious whorl of gneiss, he happened to see Mr. Long as he returned. Mr. Long came afoot, leading the sorrel horse. Just before he came within sight of camp he led the horse up beside a boulder, climbed clumsily into the saddle, clutched the saddle-horn, and so rode into camp. The act was so natural a one that Griffith, already convinced, was convinced again—the more so because Long preserved a discreet silence as to the misadventure with the sorrel horse.

Mr. Long reported profanely that the men on the other side had also been disposed to arrest him, and had been dissuaded with difficulty.

"So I guess I must look some like Bransford, though I would never 'a' guessed it. Reckon nobody knows what they really look like. Chances are a feller wouldn't know himself if he met him in the road. That squares you, kid. No hard feelings?"

"Not a bit. I certainly thought you were Bransford, at first," said Griffith.

"Well, the black-eyed one—Stone—he's coming round on the west side now, cutting sign. You be all ready to start for Escondido as soon as he gets here, Gurd. Say, you don't want to wait for the sheriff if he's up on Rainbow. You wire a lot of your friends to come on the train at nine o'clock to-night. Sheriff can come when he gets back. There ain't but a few horses at Escondido. You get Pappy Sanders to send your gang out in a wagon—such as can't find horses."

"Better take in both of ours, Gurd," said Griffith. He knew Long was all right, as has been said, but he was also newly persuaded of his own fallibility. He had been mistaken about Long being Bransford; therefore he might be mistaken about Long being Long. In this spirit of humility he made the suggestion recorded above, and was grieved that Long indorsed it.

"And I want you to do two errands for me, kid. You give this to Pappy Sanders—the storekeeper, you know"—here he produced the little eohippus from his pocket—"and tell him to send it to a jeweler for me and get a hole bored in it so it'll balance. Want to use it for a watch-charm when I get a watch. And if we pull off this Bransford affair I'll have me a watch.

167

Now don't you lose that! It's turquoise—worth a heap o' money. Besides, he's a lucky little horse."

"I'll put him in my pocketbook," said Gurdon.

"Better give him to Pappy first off, else you're liable to forget about him, he's so small. Then you tell Pappy to send me out some grub. I won't make out no bill. He's grubstakin' the mine; he'll know what to send. You just tell him I'm about out of patience. Tell him I want about everything there is, and want it quick; and a jar for sour dough—I broke mine. And get some newspapers." He hesitated perceptibly. "See here, boys, I hate to mention this; but old Pappy, him and this Jeff Bransford is purty good friends. I reckon Pappy won't much like it to furnish grub for you while you're puttin' the kibosh on Jeff. You better get some of your own. You see how it is, don't you? 'Tain't like it was my chuck."

Stone came while they saddled. He spoke apart with Griffith as to Mr. Long, and a certain favor he bore to the escaped bank-robber; but Griffith, admitting his own self-deception in that line, outlined the history of the past unhappy night. Stone, who had suffered only a slight misgiving, was fully satisfied.

As Steele started for the railroad Mr. Stone set out to complete the circuit of Double Mountain, in the which he found no runaway tracks. And Griffith and Long, sleeping alternately—especially Griffith—kept faithful ward over the gloomy gate of Double Mountain.

CHAPTER XIV

FLIGHT

"Keep away from that wheelbarrow—what the hell do you know about machinery?"   —Elbert Hubbard*

* It is not intimated that Mr. Hubbard wrote this—merely that he printed it.   —Author

JUST after dark a horseman with a led horse came jogging round the mountain on the trail from Escondido. On the led horse was a pack bound rather slouchily, not to a packsaddle, but to an old riding saddle. The horses were unwilling to enter the circle of firelight, so the rider drew rein just beyond—a slender and boyish rider, with a flopping wide-brimmed hat too large for him.

"Oh, look who's here!" said Tobe, as one who greets an unexpected friend.

"Hello, Tobe! Here's your food, grub, chuck and

169

provisions! Got your outlaw yet? Them other fellows will be out along toward midnight." He went on without waiting for an answer: "Put me on your payroll. Pappy said I was to go to work—and if you was going to quit work to hunt down his friend you'd better quit for good. Lead on to your little old mine. I don't know where it is, even."

"I'll go up and unpack, Rex," said Tobe; "but, of course, I'm not going to lose my part of that five thousand. Pappy's foolish. He's gettin' old. I'll be back after a while and bring down the papers."

Chatting of the trapped outlaw, the Ophir men climbed the zigzag to the mine. To Griffith, their voices dwindled to an indistinct murmur; a light glowed through the tent on the dump.

The stranger pressed into Jeff's hand something small and hard—the little eohippus. "Here's your little old token. Pappy caught on at once and he sent me along to represent. Let's get this pack off and get out of here. Do we have to go down the same trail again?"

"Oh, no," said Jeff. "There's a wood-trail leads round the mountain to the east. Who're you? I don't know you."

"Charley Gibson. Pappy knows me. He sent the little stone horse to vouch for me. I'm O. K. Time enough to explain when we've made a clean getaway."

"You're damn right there," Jeff said. "That boy down yonder is nobody's fool. I'll light a candle in the tent and he'll think I'm reading the newspapers. That'll hold him a while."

"I'll be going on down the trail," said Gibson. "This way, isn't it?"

"Yes, that's the one. All right. Go slow and don't make any more noise than you can help."

Jeff would have liked his own proper clothing and effects, but there was no time for resuscitation. Lighting the candle, he acquired "Alice in Wonderland" and thrust it into the bosom of his shirt. It had been years since last he read that admirable work; his way now led either to hiding or to jail—and, with Alice to share his fate, he felt equal to either fortune. He left the candle burning: the tent shone with a mellow glow.

"If he didn't hear our horses coming down we're a little bit of all right," said Jeff, as he rejoined his rescuer on the level. "Even if he does, he may think we've gone to hobble 'em—only he'd think we ought to water 'em first. Now for the way of the transgressor, to Old Mexico. This little desert'll be one busy place to-morrow!"

They circled Double Mountain, making a wide détour to avoid rough going, and riding at a hard gallop until, behind and to their right, a red spark of fire came into view from behind a hitherto intervening shoulder, marking where Stone and Harlow held the southward pass.

Jeff drew rein and bore off obliquely toward the road at an easy trot.

"They're there yet. So that's all right!" he said. "They've just put on fresh wood. I saw it flame up just then." He was in high feather. He began to laugh, or, more accurately, he resumed his laughter, for he had been too mirthful for much speech. "That poor devil Griffith will wait and fidget and stew! He'll think I'm in the tent, reading the newspapers—reading about the Arcadian bank robbery, likely. He'll wait a while, then he'll yell at me. Then he'll think we've gone to hobble the horses. He won't want to leave the gap unguarded. He won't know what to think. Finally he'll go up to the mine and see that pack piled off any which way, and no saddles. Then he'll know, but he won't know what to do. He'll think we're for Old Mexico, but he won't know it for sure. And it's too dark to track us. Oh, my stars, but I bet he'll be mad!"

.   .   .   .

Which shows that we all make mistakes. Mr. Griffith, though young, was of firm character, as has been lightly intimated. He waited a reasonable time to allow for paper-reading, then he waited a little longer and shouted; but when there was no answer he knew at once precisely what had happened: he had not been a fool at all, whatever Steele and Bransford had assured him, and he was a bigger fool to have allowed himself to be persuaded that he had been. It is true that he didn't know what was best to do, but he knew exactly what he was going to do—and did it promptly.

172

Seriously annoyed, he spurred through Double Mountain, gathered up Stone and Harlow, and followed the southward road. Bransford had been on the way to Old Mexico—he was on that road still; Griffith put everything on the one bold cast. While the others saddled he threw fresh fuel on the fire, with a rankling memory of the candle in the deserted tent and Hannibal at Saint Jo. For the first time Griffith had the better of the long battle of wits. That armful of fuel slowed Jeff from gallop to trot, turned assured victory into a doubtful contest; when the fugitives regained the El Paso road Griffith's vindictive little band was not five miles behind them.

The night was lightly clouded—not so dark but that the pursuers noticed—or thought they noticed—the fresh tracks in the road when they came to them. They stopped, struck matches and confirmed their hopes: two shod horses going south at a smart gait; the dirt was torn up too much for travelers on their lawful occasions. From that moment Griffith urged the chase unmercifully; the fleeing couple, in fancied security, lost ground with every mile.

.   .   .   .

"How on earth did you manage it? Didn't they know you?" demanded Gibson as the pace slackened.

"It wasn't me! It was Tobe Long! 'You may not have lived much under the sea, and perhaps you were never introduced to a lobster,'" quoted Jeff. Rocking in the saddle, he gave a mirthful résumé of his little envanishment, "And, oh, just think of that candle burning away in that quiet, empty tent! If I could have seen Griffith's face!" he gloated. "Oh me! Oh my! ... And he was so sure! ... Say, Gibson, how do you come in this galley?" As a lone prospector his speech had been fittingly coarse; now, with every mile, he shook off the debasing influence of Mr. Long. "Kettle-washing makes black hands. Aren't you afraid you'll get into trouble?"

"Nobody knows I'm kettle-washing, except Pappy Sanders and you," said Gibson. "I was careful not to let your friend see me at the fire."

"I'll do you a good turn sometime," said Jeff. He rode on in silence for a while and presently was lost in his own thoughts, leaning over with his hands folded on his horse's neck. In a low and thoughtful voice he half repeated, half chanted to himself:

"Illilleo Legardi, in the garden there alone,
There came to me no murmur of the fountain's under-
   tone
So mystically, magically mellow as your own!"

Another silence. Then Jeff roused himself, with a start.

"I'll tell you what, Gibson, you'd better cut loose from me. So far as I can see, you are only a kid. You don't want to get mixed up in a murder scrape. This would go pretty hard with you if they can prove it on you. Of course, I'm awfully obliged to you and all

174

that; but you'd better quit me while the quitting's good."

"Oh, no; I'll see you through," said Gibson lightly. "Besides, I know you had nothing to do with the murder."

"Oh, the hell you do!" said Jeff. "That's kind of you, I'm sure. See here, who'd sold you your chips anyway? How'd you get in this game?"

"I got in this game, as you put it, because I jolly well wanted to," replied Charley, with becoming spirit. "That ought to be reason enough for anything in this country. Nothing against it in the rules—and I don't use the rules, anyhow. If you must have it all spelled out for you—I knew, or at least I'd heard, that your friends were away from Rainbow; so I judged you wouldn't go up there. Then I knew those four amateur Sherlocks—they're in my set in Arcadia. When two of the deerhunters, after starting at two A.M., came back to Arcadia the same morning they left, looking all wise and important, and slipped off on the train to Escondido, saying nothing to any one— and when the other two didn't come home at all—I began to think; went down to the depot, found they had gone to Escondido, and I came on the next train. I found out Pappy was your friend; and when he got your little hurry-up call I volunteered my services, seeing Pappy was too old and not footloose anyhow— with a wife and property. That's the how of it."

"Oh, yes, that's all right; but what makes you think I'm innocent?"

175

"I know Mr. White, you see. And Mr. White seems to think that at about the time the bank was robbed you were—in a garden!" Charley's voice was edged with faint mockery.

"Huh!" said Jeff, startled. "Who in hell is Mr. White?"

"Mr. White—in hell—is the devil!" said Charley.

At this unexpected disclosure Jeff lashed his horse to a gallop—his spurs, you remember, being certain feet under the Ophir dump—and strove to bring his thoughts to bear upon this new situation. He slowed down and Charley drew up beside him.

"You seem to have stayed quite a while—in a garden," suggested Charley.

"That tongue of yours is going to get you into trouble yet," said Jeff. "You'll never live to be gray-headed."

Charley was not to be daunted.

"Say, Jeff, she's pretty easy to get acquainted with, what? And those eyes of hers—a little on the see-you-later style, aren't they?"

Jeff turned in his saddle.

"Now you look here, Mr. Charley Gibson! I'm under obligations to you, and so on—but I've heard all of that kind of talk that's good—*sabe?*"

"Oh, I know her," persisted Charley. "Know her by heart—know her like a book. She made a fool of me, too. She drives 'em single, double, tandem, random and four abreast!"

"You little beast!" Jeff launched his horse at the traducer, but Gibson spurred aside.

"Stop now, Jeffy! Easy does it! I've got a gun!"

"Shut your damn head then! Gun or no gun, don't you take that girl's name in your mouth again, or——Hark! What's that?"

It was a clatter far behind—a ringing of swift hoofs on hard ground.

"By George, they're coming! Griffith will be a man yet!" said Jeff approvingly. "Come on, kid; we've got to burn the breeze! I suppose that talk of yours is only your damn fool idea of fun, but I don't like it. Cut it out, now, and ride like a drunk Indian!" He laughed loud and long. "Think o' that candle, will you?—burning away with a clear, bright, steady flame, and nobody within ten miles of it!"

They raced side by side; but Gibson, heedless of their perilous situation, or perhaps taking advantage of it, took a malicious delight in goading Jeff to madness; and he refused either to be silent or to talk about candles, notwithstanding Jeff's preference for that topic.

"I'm not joking! I'm telling you for your own good." Here the tormentor prudently fell back half a length and raised his voice so as to be heard above the flying feet. "Hasn't she gone back to New York, I'd like to know, and left you to get out of it the best way you can? She could 'a' stayed if she'd wanted to. Don't tell me! Haven't I seen how she bosses her mother

177

round? No, sir! She's willing to let you hang to save herself a little slander—or, more likely, a little talk!"

Jeff whirled his horse to his haunches, but once more Gibson was too quick for him. Gibson's horse was naturally the nimbler of the two, even without the advantage of spurs.

"That's a lie! She was going to tell—she was bound to tell; I made her keep silent. After I jumped out she couldn't well say anything. That's why I jumped. Was I going to make her a target for such vile tongues as yours—for me? Oh! You ought to be shot out of a red-hot cannon, through a barbed-wire fence, into hell! You lie, you coward, you know you lie! I'll cram it down your throat if you'll get off and throw that gun down!"

"Yah! It's likely I'll put the gun down!" scoffed Gibson. "Ride on, you fool! Do you want to hang? Ride on and keep ahead! Remember, I've got the gun!"

"Hanging's not so bad," snarled Jeff. "I'd rather be hung decently than be such a thing as you! Oh, if I just had a gun!"

The sound of pursuit was clearer now; and, of course, the pursuers could hear the pursued as well and fought for every inch.

Jeff rode on, furious at his helplessness. For several miles his tormentor raced behind in silence, fearing, if he persisted longer in his evil course, that Jeff would actually stop and give himself up. They gained

178

now on their pursuers, who had pressed their horses overhard to make up the five-mile handicap.

As they came to a patch of sandy ground they eased the pace somewhat. Charley drew a little closer to Jeff.

"Now don't get mad. I had no idea you thought so much of the girl——"

"Shut up, will you?"

"——or I wouldn't have deviled you so. I'll quit. How was I to know you'd stop to fight for her with the very rope round your neck? It's a pity she'll never know about it. . . . You can't have seen her more than two or three times—and Heaven only knows where that was! On that camping trip, I reckon. What kind of a girl is she, anyhow, to hold clandestine interviews with a stranger? . . . She'll write to you by and by—a little scented note, with a little stilted, meaningless word of thanks. No, she won't. It'll be gushy: 'Oh, my hero! How can I ever repay you?' She won't let you out of her clutches—anybody, so long as it's a man! Here! None o' that! . . . Go on, now, if you want to live!"

"Who the hell wants to live?"

A noose flew back from the darkness. Jeff's horse darted aside and Gibson was jerked sprawling to the sand at a rope's end—hat flew one way, gun another. Jeff ran to the six-shooter.

"Who's got the gun now?" he jeered, as he loosened the rope. "I only wish we had two of 'em!"

"You harebrained idiot!" Charley grabbed up his

179

hat and spit sand from his mouth. "Get your horse and ride, you unthinkable donkey!"

"Pleasure first, business afterward!" Jeff unbuckled Gibson's gunbelt and transferred it to his own waist, jerking Gibson to his feet in the violent process. "Now, you little blackguard, you either take back all that or you'll get the lickin' o' your life! You're too small; but all the same——"

"Oh, I'll take it back, you big bully—all I said and a lot more I only thought!" said Charley spitefully. He was almost crying with rage as he limped to his horse. "She's an angel on earth! Sure she is! Ride, you maniac—ride! Oh, you ought to be hung! I hope you do hang—you miserable ruffian!"

The following hoofs no longer rang sharply; they took on a muffled beat—they were in the sand's edge not a mile behind.

"Ride ahead, you! I've got the gun, remember!" observed Jeff significantly; "but if you slur that girl again I'll not shoot you—I'll naturally wear you out with this belt."

CHAPTER XV

GOOD-BY

"They have ridden the low moon out of the sky; their hoofs drum up the dawn."   —*Two Strong Men*, Kipling

"I'M not speaking of her and I'm not going to," protested Gibson, in a changed tone. "I'll promise! My horse is failing, Jeff. I rode hard and fast from Escondido. Your horse carried nothing much but a saddle— that pack was mostly bluff, you know. And those fellows' horses have come twenty miles less than either of ours."

No answer.

"I don't believe we're going to make it, Jeff!" There was a forlorn little quaver in Charley's voice.

Jeff grunted. "Uh! Maybe not. Griffith'll be real pleased."

Gibson rode closer. "Can't we turn off the road and hide?"

"Till daylight," said Jeff. "Then they'll get us. No way out of this desert except across the edges somewhere. You go if you want to. They won't bother to hunt for you, maybe, if they get me."

"No. It's my fault. . . . I'll see it out. . . . I'm sorry, Jeff—but it was so funny!" Here, rather to Jeff's surprise, Charley's dejection gave place to laughter.

They rode up a sandy slope where mesquites grew black along the road. Blown sand had lodged to hummocks in their thick and matted growth; the road was a sunken way.

"How far is it from here, Jeff?"

"Ten miles—maybe only eight—to the river. We're in Texas now—have been for an hour."

"Think we can make it?"

"*Quien sabe?*"

Gibson drew rein. "You go on. Your horse isn't so tired."

"Oh, I guess not!" said Jeff. "Come on."

The sound of pursuit came clear through the quiet night. There was silence for a little.

"What'll you do, Jeff? Fight?"

"I can't!" said Jeff. "Hurt those boys? I couldn't fight, the way it is—hardly, even if 'twas the sheriff. I'll just hang, I reckon."

They reached the top of the little slope and turned down the other side.

"I don't altogether like this hanging idea," said

Gibson. "I got you into this, Jeff; so I'll just get you out again—like the man in our town who was so wondrous wise. Going to use bramble bushes, too." Volatile Gibson, in the stress of danger, had forgotten his wrath. He was light-hearted and happy, frivolously gay. "Give me your rope and your gun, Jeff. Quick now! No, I won't mention your girl—not once! Hurry!"

"What you going to do?" asked Jeff, thoroughly mystified.

"Ever read the 'Fool's Errand'?" Charley chuckled. "No? Well, I have. Jump off and tie the end of your rope to that mesquite root. Quick!"

He sprang down, snatched one end of the coil from Jeff's hand and stretched it taut across the road, a foot from the ground. "Now your gun! Quick!"

He snatched the gun, tied an end of his own saddle-rope to the stretched one, near the middle, plunged through the mesquite, over a hummock, paying out his rope as he went; wedged the gun firmly in the springing crotch of a mesquite tree, cocked it and tied the loose end of the trailing rope to the trigger. He ran back and sprang on his horse.

"Now ride! It's our last chance!"

"Kid, you're a wonder!" said Jeff. "You'll do to take along! They'll lope up when they turn down that slope, hit that rope and pile in a heap!"

"And my rope will fire the gun off!" shrilled joyous Charley. "They'll think it's us—an ambuscade——"

"They'll take to the sandhills," Jeff broke in.

183

"They'll shoot into the bushes—they'll think it's us firing back, half the time. . . . They'll scatter out and surround that lonesome, harmless motte and watch it till daylight. You bet they won't go projecting round it any till daylight, either!" He looked up at the sky. "There's the morning star. See it? 'They have ridden the low moon out of the sky'—only there isn't any moon—'their hoofs drum up the dawn.' Then they'll find our tracks—and if I only could see the captain's face! 'Oh, my threshings, and the corn of my floor!' . . . And by then we'll be in Mexico and asleep. . . . When Griffith finds that gun—oh, he'll never show his head in Arcadia again! . . . Say, Charley, I hope none of 'em get hurt when they strike your skip-rope."

"Huh! It's sandy! A heap you cared about me getting hurt when you dragged me from my horse!" said Gibson, rather snappishly. "You did hurt me, too. You nearly broke my neck and you cut my arms. And I got full of mesquite thorns when I set that gun. You don't care! I'm only the man that came to save your neck. That's the thanks I get! But the men that are trying to hang you—that's different! You'd better go back. They might get hurt. You'll be sorry sometime for the way you've treated me. There—it's too late now!"

A shot rang behind them. There was a brief silence. Then came a sharp fusillade, followed by scattering shots, dwindling to longer intervals.

Jeff clung to his saddlehorn.

"I guess they ain't hurt much," he laughed. "Wish

I could see 'em when they find out! Slow down, kid. We've got lots of time now."

"We haven't," protested Charley. "Keep moving. It's hard on the horses, but they'll have a lifetime to rest in. They've telegraphed all over the country. You want to cross the river before daylight. It would be too bad for you to be caught now! Is there any ford, do you know?"

"Not this time of year. River's up."

"Cross in a boat then?"

"Guess we'd better. That horse of yours is pretty well used up. Don't believe he could swim it."

"Oh, I'm not going over. I'll get up to El Paso. I've got friends there."

"You'll get caught."

"No, I won't. I'm not going across, I tell you, and that's all there is to it! I guess I'll have something to say about things. I'm going to see you safely over, and that's the last you'll ever see of Charley Gibson."

"Oh, well!" Jeff reflected a little. "If you're sure you won't come along, I'd rather swim. My horse is strong yet. You see, it takes time to find a boat, and a boat means a house and dogs; and I'll need my horse on the other side. How'll you get to El Paso? Griffith'll likely come down here about an hour by sun, 'cross lots, a-cryin'."

"I'll manage that," said Gibson curtly enough. "You tend to your own affair."

"Oh, all right!" Jeff rode ahead. He whistled; then he chanted his war song:

"Said the little Eohippus:
  'I'm going to be a horse!
And on my middle fingernails
  To run my earthly course!'
The Coryphodon was horrified;
  The Dinoceras was shocked;
And they chased young Eohippus,
  But he skipped away and mocked.

"Said they: 'You always were as small
  And mean as now we see,
And that's conclusive evidence
  That you're always going to be.
What! Be a great, tall, handsome beast,
  With hoofs to gallop on?
Why! You'd have to change your nature!'
  Said the Loxolophodon."

"Jeff!"

"Well?" Jeff turned his head. Charley was drooping visibly.

"Stop that foolish song!"

Jeff rode on in silence. This was a variable person, Gibson. They were dropping down from the mesa into the valley of the Rio Grande.

"Jeff!"

Jeff fell back beside Charley. "Tired, pardner?"

"Jeff, I'm terribly tired! I'm not used to riding so far; and I'm sleepy—so sleepy!"

"All right, pardner; we'll go slower. We'll walk. Most there now. There's the railroad."

"Keep on trotting. I can stand it. We must get to the

river before daylight. Is is far?" Charley's voice was weary. The broad sombrero drooped sympathetically.

"Two miles to the river. El Paso's seven or eight miles up the line. Brace up, old man! You've done fine and dandy! It's just because the excitement is all over. Why should you go any farther, anyhow? There's Ysleta up the track a bit. Follow the road up there and flag the first train. That'll be best."

"No, no. I'll go all the way. I'll make out." Charley straightened himself with an effort.

They crossed the Espee tracks and came to a lane between cultivated fields.

"Jeff! I'd like to say something. It won't be breaking my promise really. . . . I didn't mean what I said about—you know. I was only teasing. She's a good enough girl, I guess—as girls go."

Jeff nodded. "I did not need to be told that."

"And you left her in a cruel position when you jumped out of the window. She *can't* tell now, so long as there's any other way. What a foolish thing to do! If you'd just said at first that you were in the garden—— Oh, why didn't you? But after the chances you took rather than to tell—why, Jeff, it would be terrible for her now."

"I know that, too," said Jeff. "I suppose I was a fool; but I didn't want her to get mixed up with it, and at the same time I cared less about hanging than any time I can remember. You see, I didn't know till the last minute that the garden was going to cut any figure. And do you suppose I'd have that courthouseful of fools buzzing and whispering at her? Not much! Maybe it was foolish—but I'm glad I did it."

"I'm glad of it, too. If you had to be a fool," said Charley, "I'm glad you were that kind of a fool. Are you still mad at me?"

Since Charley had recanted, and more especially since he had taken considerate thought for the girl's compulsory silence, Jeff's anger had evaporated.

"That's all right, pardner. . . . Only you oughtn't never to talk that way about a girl—even for a joke. That's no good kind of a joke. Men, now, that's different. See here, I'll give you an order to a fellow in El Paso—Hibler—to pay for your horses and your gun. Here's your belt, too."

Charley shook his head impatiently. "I don't want any money. Settle with Pappy for the horses. I won't take this one back. Keep the belt. You may want it to beat me with sometime. What are you going to do, Jeff? Aren't you ever coming back?"

"Sure I'll come back—if only to see Griffith again. I'll write to John Wesley Pringle—he's my mainest side pardner—and sick him on to find out who robbed that bank—to prove it, rather. I just about almost nearly know who it was. Old Wes'll straighten things out a-flying. I'll be back in no time. I got to come back, Charley!"

The river was in sight. The stars were fading; there was a flush in the east, a smell of dawn in the air.

"Jeff, I wish you'd do something for me."

"Sure, Charley. What is it?"

"I wish you'd give me that little turquoise horse to remember you by."

Jeff was silent for a little. He had framed out another plan for the little eohippus—namely, to give him to Miss Ellinor. He sighed; but he owed a good deal to Charley.

"All right, Charley. Take good care of him—he's a lucky little horse. I think a heap of him. Here we are!"

The trees were distinct in the growing light. Jeff rode into the river; the muddy water swirled about his horse's knees. He halted for parting; Gibson rode in beside him. Jeff took the precious Alice book from his bosom, put it in the crown of his miner's cap and jammed the cap tightly on his head.

"Better change your mind, Charley. Come along. We'll rout somebody out and order a dish of stewed eggs.

"There is another shore, you know, upon the other side.
The farther off from England the nearer 'tis to France;
Then turn not pale, beloved snail, but come and join the
    dance.
Will you—won't you——"

" 'No, I won't! I told you once!' " snapped the beloved snail.

"Here's the little eohippus horse then." As Charley took it Jeff wrung his hand. "By George, I've got to change my notion of Arcadia people. If there's many like you and Griffith, Arcadia's going to crowd the map! ... Well—so long!"

"It looks awful wide, Jeff!"

"Oh, I'll be all right—swim it myself if the horse plays out—and if I don't have no cramps, as I might, of course, after this ride. Well—here goes nothin'! Take care of the little horse. I hope he brings you good luck!"

"Well—so long, then!"

Bransford rode into the muddy waters. They came to the horse's breast, his neck; he plunged in, sank, rose, and was borne away down the swift current, breasting the flood stoutly—and so went quartering across to the farther bank. It took a long time. It was quite light when the horse found footing on a sandbar half a mile below, rested, and splashed whitely through the shallows to the bank. Gibson swung his sombrero. Jeff waved his hand, rode to the fringing bushes, and was gone.

CHAPTER XVI

THE LAND OF AFTERNOON

"Dreaming once more love's old sad dream divine."

LOS BAÑOS DE SANTA EULALIA DEL NORTE, otherwise known as Mud Springs, is a Mexican hamlet, with one street of about the same length. Los Baños—all that— lies in an ox-bow of the Rio Grande, half a day in mere miles from El Paso; otherwise a contemporary of Damascus and Arpad.

Thither, mindful of the hot springs which supply the preliminaries of the name, went Mr. Bransford. A stranger to the border custom might have simulated illness as an excuse for a modest life, and so retired from public view—in which case there would have been whisperings; but Jeff was in their bosoms, bone of their bone; he cunningly gave it out that he was from the American side, a fugitive with a price upon

191

his head. Suspicion thus disarmed, he became the guest of the city.

Observe now how Nature insists upon averages. Mr. Jeff Bransford was, as has been seen, an energetic man; but outraged nerves will have their revenge. After making proper amends to his damaged eye Jeff's remnant of energy kept up long enough to dispatch young Tomás Escobar y Mendoza to El Paso with a message to Hibler: which message enjoined Hibler at once to carry tidings to John Wesley Pringle, somewhere in Chihuahua, asking him kindly to set right what Arcadian times were out of joint, as he, Jeff, felt the climate of Old Mexico more favorable for his throat trouble than that of New Mexico, with a postscript asking Hibler for money by bearer. And young Tomás was instructed to buy a complete outfit of clothing for Jeff at Juarez.

This done the reaction set in—aided, perhaps, by the enervating lassitude of the hot baths and the sleepy atmosphere of that forgotten village. Jeff spent the better part of a fortnight asleep—or half awake at best. He had pleasant dreams too. One—perhaps the best-liked—was that on their wedding trip they should follow again the devious line of his flight from Arcadia. That would need a prairie schooner—no, a prairie steamboat—a prairie yacht! He would tell her all the hideous details—show her the mine, the camp of the besiegers, the ambuscade on the road. And if he could only have Ellinor meet Griffith and Gibson for a crowning touch!

After the strenuous violence of handstrokes here was a drowsy and peaceful time. The wine of that land was good, the shade pleasant, the Alician philosophy more delightful than of yore; he had all the accessories but one of an earthly paradise. Man is ungrateful. Jeff was a man; neglectful of present bounties, his dreaming thoughts were all of the absent accessory and of a time when that absence should be no more, nor paradise be empty.

Life, like the Gryphon's classical master, had taught him Laughter and Grief. He turned now the forgotten pages of the book of his years. Enough black pages were there, as you will know well, having yourself searched old records before now with tears. He cast up that long account—the wasted lendings, the outlawed debts, the dishonored promises, the talents of his stewardship, unprofitable and brought to naught; set down—how gladly!—the items on the credit side. So men have set the good upon one side and the evil on the other since Crusoe's day, and before; against the time when the Great Accountant, Whose values are not ours, shall strike a final balance.

Take that book at your elbow—yes, either one; it doesn't matter. Now turn to where the hero first discovers his frightful condition—long after it has become neighborhood property. . . . He bent his head in humility. He was not worthy of her! . . . Something like that? Those may not be the precise words; but he groaned. He always groans. By-the-way, how this man-saying must amuse womankind! Yes, and they

193

really say it too—real, live, flesh-and-blood men. Who was it said life was a poor imitation of literature? Happily they either are insincere or they reconsider the matter—else what should we do for families?

It is to be said that Jeff Bransford lacked this becoming delicacy. If he groaned he swore also; but if he decided that Miss Ellinor Hoffman deserved a better man than he was he also highly resolved that she should not have him.

"For, after all, you know," said Jeff to Alice:

" 'I'm sure he's nothing extra—a quiet man and plain,
And modest—though there isn't much of which he could
be vain.
And, had I mind to chant his praise, this were the kindest
line—
Somehow, she loves him dearly—this little love of
mine!' "

Yet was it that? Would it not be gratitude that he had taken a little risk for her—he who loved risk for the very joy of danger? Just now she would be thinking him quite a wonderful person—him, Jeff Bransford! That shine would wear off. Had it not been at first merely a girl's romantic fancy, the fascination of the unknown, because his way of life was new and strange to her—because he was a little different, perhaps, from the men she had known? . . . He must be sure. He must not wrong her; must not let her make a mistake and find it out too late. . . . Events had been his accomplices; the stars in their courses had fought for him; the glamour of adventure had swept her from

194

her feet; she must give herself now or feel herself ungrateful, false. . . . The advantage was all with him. If
he could meet her again on even terms, like the others;
if she met him as a stranger; if he could court her anew
from the first; if, when she came to know him well in
the sober, workaday world—that would be a different
thing. The thought shaped and grew; he brooded on it.

.   .   .   .

Johnny Dines rode with a pleasant jingle down the
shady street of Los Baños de Santa Eulalia del Norte.
His saddle was new, carved, wrought with silver; his
bridle shone as the sun, his spurs as bright stars; he
shed music from his feet. Jeff saw him turn to Casa
Escobar: apple blossoms made a fragrant lane for
him. He paused at Jeff's tree.

"*Alto allí!*" said Johnny. The words, as sharp command, can be managed in two brisk syllables. The
sound is then: "*Altwaí!*" It is a crisp and startling
sound, and the sense of it in our idiom is: "Hands up!"
Jeff had been breakfasting *al fresco*; he made glad
room on his bench. "Light, stranger, and look at your
saddle! Pretty slick saddle too. Guess your playmates
must 'a' went home talking to themselves last night."

"They're going to kill a maverick for you at Arcadia
and give a barbecue," said Johnny. The cult of *nil
admirari* reaches its highest pitch of prosperity in the
cow-countries, and Johnny knew that it was for him
to broach tidings unasked.

"Oh, that reminds me—how's old Lars Porsena?" said Jeff, now free to question.

"Him? He's all right," said Johnny casually. "Goin' to marry one or more of the nurses. They're holdin' elimination contests now."

"Say, Johnny, when you go back wish you'd tell him I didn't do it. Cross my heart and hope to die if I did!"

"Oh, he knows that!" said Johnny.

Jeff shook his head doubtfully.

"Evidence was pretty strong—pretty strong. Who was it then?"

"Why, Lake himself—old hog!"

"If Lake keeps on like this he's going to have people down on him," said Jeff. "Who did the Holmesing— John Wesley?"

"Oh, John Wesley! John Wesley!" said Dines scornfully. "You think the sun rises and sets in old John Wesley Pringle. Naw; he didn't get back till it was all over. I cannot tell a lie. I did it with my little hatchet!"

"Must have had it sharpened up!" said Jeff. "Tell it to me!"

"Why, there isn't much to tell," said Dines, suddenly modest. "Come to think of it, I had right considerable help. There was a young college chap—he first put it into my head that it wasn't you."

"That would be the devil?" said Jeff, ignoring the insult.

196

"Just so. Name's White—and so's he: Billy White, S. M. and G. P."

"I don't just remember them degrees," said Jeff.

"Aw, keep still and you'll hear more. They stand for Some Man and Good People. Well, as I was a-saying, Billy he seemed to think it wasn't you. He stuck to it that Buttinski—that's what he calls you— was in a garden just when the bank was robbed."

Johnny contemplated the apple tree over his head. It was a wandering and sober glance, but a muscle twitched in his cheek—and he made no further explanation about the garden.

"And then I remembered about Nigger Babe throwin' you off, and I began to think maybe you didn't crack the safe after all. And there was some other things—little things—that made Billy and Jimmy Phillips—he was takin' cards in the game too —made 'em think maybe it was Lake; but it wasn't no proof—not to say proof. And there's where I come in."

"Well?" said Jeff as Johnny paused.

"Simple enough, once you knowed how," said Johnny modestly. "I'd been reading lots of them detective books—Sherlock Holmes and all them fellows. I got Billy to have his folks toll Lake's sister away for the night, so she wouldn't be scared. Then me and Billy and Jimmy Phillips and Monte, we broke in and blowed up Lake's private safe. No trouble at all. Since the bank-robbin' every one had been tellin' round just how it ought to be done—crackin' safes. Funny how a fellow picks up little scraps of useful knowledge like

197

that—things you'd think he'd remember might come in handy most any time—and then forgets all about 'em. I wrote it down this time. Won't forget it again."

"Well?" said Jeff again.

"Oh, yes. And there was the nice money—all the notes and all the gold he could tote."

Jeff's eye wandered to the new saddle.

"I kept some of the yellow stuff as a souvenir— half a quart, or maybe a pint," said Johnny. "I don't want no reward for doin' a good deed. . . . And that's all."

"Lake is a long, ugly word," said Jeff thoughtfully.

"Well, what do you say?" prompted Johnny.

"Oh, thank you, thank you!" said Jeff. "You showed marvelous penetration—marvelous! But say, Johnny, if the money hadn't been there wouldn't that have been awkward?"

"Oh, Billy was pretty sure Lake was the man. And we figured he hadn't bothered to move it—you being the goat that way. What made you be a goat, Jeff?"

"On the contrary, what made your Billy think it was Lake?"

Johnny told him in detail.

"Pretty good article of plain thinking, wasn't it?" he concluded. "Yet he mightn't have got started on the right track at all if he hadn't had a tip about your bein' in a garden." Johnny's eye reverted to the apple tree.

"Mr. J. Dines, I've been thinking ——" Jeff began.

Johnny glanced at him anxiously.

"—— and I've about come to the conclusion that we're some narrow contracted and bigoted on Rainbow. We don't know it all! We ain't the only pebble! From what I've seen of these Arcadia men they seem to be pretty good stuff—and like as not it's just the same way all along the beach. There's your Mr. White, and Griffith, and Gibson—did I tell you about Gibson?"

Johnny flashed a smile. His smiles always looked larger than they really were, because Johnny was so small.

"I saw Griffith and he gave me his version—several times. He's real upset, Griffith. . . . Last time he told me he leaned up against my neck and wept copious because there was only ten commandments!"

"Didn't see Gibson, did you? You know him?"

"Nope. Pappy picked him up—or he picked Pappy up rather. Hasn't been seen since. That reminds me, Jeff. I might have been down here sooner, quick as Wes' come back and told me where you was; but I thought you might want your mail. So I stopped off at Escondido—a few days. I wasn't sure at first—looked like a man's handwrite; but when the last one come I knew by the postmark it was her. Here you are."

He tossed four letters on the table—four bulky ones. One bore the datemark of the railroad postal service; one was from Kansas City; one from Chicago—and the last and thickest one was dated at Owecum, New York.

"I've a good mind to kill you!" said Jeff.

199

"You two kids," said Johnny severely, "remind me of Wildcat Thompson's powder story: 'Well, sir,' says Wildcat, 'well, sir, this here feller he lit a cigarette an' throwed away the match, an' it fell in a powder kaig; an' do you know more'n half that powder burned up before they could put it out!' "

"I will kill you!" said Jeff.

.   .   .   .

"Johnny," said Jeff later, "I ain't going back to Rainbow."

"I was afraid you wouldn't—now," said Johnny rather soberly. "Jeff, you can kick me after I say my little piece—but ain't you afraid you may be making a mistake? That girl now—nice girl, and all that—but that girl's got money, Jeff. She's got no business marryin' a poor man, with her raisin'. And a poor man's got no business to marry her."

"Oh, I'm not poor," said Jeff lightly. "I got money to throw at the birds—all kinds of money. Got a fifty-one per cent interest in a copper mine over in Arizona that's been payin' me all the way from ten to fifteen thousand clear per each and every year for the last seven years, besides what I pay a lad for lookout to keep anybody but himself from stealing any of it. He's been buyin' real estate for me in Los Angeles lately."

Johnny's jaw dropped in unaffected amazement.

"All this while? Before you hit Rainbow?"

200

"Sure!" said Jeff.

"And you workin' for forty a month and stealin' your own beef?—then saving up and buying your little old brand along with Beebe and Leo and old Wes', joggin' along, workin' like a yaller dog with fleas?"

"Why not? Wasn't I having a heap of fun? Where can I see any better time than I had here, or find better friends? Money's no good by itself. I haven't drawn a dollar from Arizona since I left. It was fun to make the mine go round at first; but when it got so it'd work I looked for something else more amusing."

"I should think you'd want to travel anyhow."

"Travel?" echoed Jeff. "Travel? Why, you dam' fool, I'm here now!"

"Why don't you stay here then?" Johnny veered from his first position. They would miss Jeff on Rainbow.

"I'm going to trust you, Johnny. Not a word, even to Wes'. You're young—you'll understand. I'm going back to New York. First, I'm going to Arizona for two or three months, grow a Vandyke and eyeglasses, manicure my nails and practice the king's English."

"What's that for? I make ten mistakes talkin' where you do one; but I get my meals."

"That's because you talk ten times as much as I do. And when the dinky little beard gets long enough I'm going back to New York then, to get—uh—to find— to see——"

"To see the gardens! Oh, yes. What figure does the

201

beard cut and the little old gold-rimmed specs? Going to wear 'em with a black cord?"

"Why, don't you understand? I'm not going to be Jeff Bransford—some one else. Tommy—let me see now—Tommy! Tommy what?"

"It does sound affectionate," said Johnny. "Tommy! Tom—mie." He experimented with the name several times with varied but tender inflection. "But you can't make it stick, Jeff."

"Tommy West, of course!" said Jeff triumphantly. Then he returned to the point at issue, "Oh, yes, I can. She's never seen me but twice—and once I was masked."

"Yes—I know." Johnny's eye rolled provokingly to the apple blossoms. "Lake found your mask, you know, where you left it. To give him his due, Lake didn't tell—I'll say that for him. I reckon maybe he saw you when he went too. Careless! Jeff, how long——"

Jeff interrupted:

"So I want you to manage my mail. Send it to Ed Dowlin at Denver. He'll forward it to me under cover, wherever I am. Then I'll send the letters I write to you—some of 'em—with the inside envelope addressed the way I want it—and sealed, Mr. Dines—sealed! D'ye understand? Then you mail 'em for me at Escondido and keep a shut head. Not a peep from you, remember!"

"Aw, what you want to do all that for? Don't be a dam' fool. Why don't you go on back there now? If you're going to quit us quit us cold and be done with it. She'll know you anyhow! What's the bally use of all this skulduddery?"

" ' "Why with an M?" said Alice. "Why not?" said the March Hare.' " Jeff shoved the Alice book across the breakfast table with a bow. "J. Dines, I hereby present you with this little volume as a slight recognition of your many services. Take it and be happy! It will answer any question as truthfully as you wish. For example, to your highly impertinent query it gave the decisive reply: 'Why not?' This skulduddery, as you are pleased to call it, is to be done because I want to do it. Why not? There ain't any why not! Exit Jeff Bransford—enter Tommy West, all dressed in clothes. You'll find full justification for it in the book. 'If it had grown up it would have been a dreadfully ugly child; but it makes rather a handsome pig, I think.' I've got it all figured out. When did you ever know me to fall down on anything I seriously undertook to do? I'll go through with this if it takes eleven innings."

"You can't do it," said Johnny. "Aw, cut it out, Jeff!"

Jeff set his mouth stubbornly.

"I'm going to be a horse, I tell you!"

"I should say," said Johnny Dines, "that it was highly improbable."

203

Chapter XVII

TWENTIETH CENTURY

> "And there that hulking Prejudice
> Sat all across the road.
>
> . . . .
> I took my hat, I took my coat,
> My load I settled fair,
> I approached that awful incubus
> With an absent-minded air—
> And I walked directly through him
> As if he wasn't there !"
>
> —*An Obstacle*
> CHARLOTTE PERKINS STETSON

"ABSOLUTE idealism," said the Idealist, "assigns ultimate reality only to the unity consisting of both object and consciousness in indissoluble correlation. It
denies the existence of reality independent of consciousness."

More, also, he said, which was promptly and oft-times simultaneously denied by the Empiricist. While they say it we will look round.

The railroad hugged the east shore of Lake Cayuga, pinched between water and overhanging hill. Traffic was suspended. Along the railroad marched a lock-stepping army, four abreast and four miles long, that being the distance between Ithaca and Portland Point. It was only three in the afternoon, and at sundown Cornell was to race with—never mind. We would not wittingly hurt the feelings of any university. At sundown there were to be two events—Varsity and Freshman. Hence the army. The sky was cloudless and the sun was hot, but the army was happy. I do not know why.

The column had been marching for ages, ever debouching to line the lake shore and the railway embankment from McKinney's to Portland Point—but never diminishing. The observation train, twenty-seven cars of beauty and chivalry—especially chivalry—had gone up early; for experience had proved that a train could not run satisfactorily when the army held the track: after running over just about so many people, the driving wheels would slip unless the rails were constantly sanded.

On the lake opposite McKinney's were schools, shoals, swarms of watercraft, steamers, schooners, catboats, motor boats, scows, tugs, tubs, catamarans, canoes, rafts; one governor's yacht, sent from Albany by mail at the request of grateful taxpayers; and one bustling, busy and consciously important police boat, flashing up and down the course in frantic, vain but happy effort to keep a wide clear lane for the shells at the finish—for the race was only three or four hours away.

A highway ran along a shelf on the hillside, a hundred feet above the railroad, and along it crept a dusty double line of autos. Between highway and railway were tiny jutting promontories. These, the choice seats for the thrilling drama, were occupied by the early settlers.

One such promontory, secluded and shady, was occupied by philosophy, the subtrahend of a once marvelous lunch, the Owecum can of "townies," and Mr. T. West, born Bransford; the latter having been perpetrated upon Stewart by Sophomore Johnny McCourt, of Heart's Disease, New Mexico. The foisting of Mr. West upon the party had been a most unjustifiable proceeding on the part of Mr. McCourt, who had a mere calling acquaintance with Stewart, dating from a little poker party the night before. However, McCourt had been insistent and hasty; mumbling something indistinctly about "good fellow," "stranger here" and "prior engagement," he had fairly thrust Mr. West into Mr. Stewart's arms—and, paying no heed to Stewart's protest that he, too, had a date for the day with a big bunch of philosophers and philanderers, had straightway made his escape, having forced Mr. West as a juggler forces a card.

Mr. West, in this false situation, had endeavored

with many apologies to relieve Mr. Stewart of this embarrassing demand upon hospitality—not mentioning that young Mr. McCourt's rudeness had been of his own elaborate designing. Stewart, however, a good fellow himself, had overridden Mr. West's scruples and brought him along. Nor had he regretted it. Mr. West, though much older than the others of the party, had evinced an admirable spice of deviltry, giving loyal aid to Stewart's joyous philosopher-baiting—a diversion that had amused the baiters and had disconcerted the philosophers no more than the crackling of thorns under a pot.

As for the philanderers and philanthropists, one pair, Miss Esther Needham and Mr. Earl Freeman, had noted not philosophers, ribald critics, dust, heat, Lake Cayuga—nor even lunch itself. The other couple, Miss Ellinor Hoffman and the Pragmatist, could not justly be called phil-anything, for Miss Hoffman was merely civil in her own cordial way; and, as every one knows, pragmatism is hardly worthy the name of philosophy at all, being mere systematic common-sense, and being further degraded by a forming desire to get somewhere—which low practical desire for results alone distinguishes it from simple empiricism.

Meanwhile the discussion got no "forrarder."

"The concept," continued the Idealist, "is a vassal in epistemology, lacking all autonomy; you can take out of it only what you first put into it through perception."

"There are more strange things in your philosophy than are dreamed of in Heaven or earth—or elsewhere," said Stewart. "If I get you, Locke proved the non-existence of ideas; Berkeley demonstrated that the existence of matter cannot be proved and knocked out the mistaken belief in the existence of self. You are all agreed only in a brutal prejudice against guessing. Then, dearly beloved, the question arises, Where are we at? If we are not ourselves are we mere probabilities? Who and why are we?"

"We are just part of the Red King's dream," said Mr. West. " ' "And what good came of it at last?" quoth little Peterkin.' "

" 'When Bishop Berkeley said there was no matter, and proved it was no matter—what he said.' " This murmured contribution was from the Pragmatist.

"Are we to put in all our lives deciding as to whether and how we can think, and never really think?" demanded Stewart. "I tell you, if you fellows had been building the Erie Canal, you wouldn't have the first mile of it surveyed yet. You would be arguing still as to whether there could be any such thing as a point, a line or a level."

The Idealist looked at, over and by them with all the large tolerance with which Goliath of Gath might have viewed the ferocious onslaught of a mouse.

"Hegel settles once for all the question of the organic nature of thought and judgment. Allow me to quote: 'It is a mistake to imagine——' "

"Aw, cut it out now! Sing us Tarpaulin Jacky—

there's a dear!" implored Stewart; but the Idealist was unmoved.

" '——to imagine that the objects which form the content of our mental ideas come first and that our subjective agency then supervenes, and by the aforesaid operation of abstraction, and by colligating the points possessed in common by the objects, frames notions of them. Rather the notion is the genuine first; and things are what they are through the action of the notion immanent in them and revealing itself in them.' "

"That settles it! Self-preservation is the first law of Nature," announced Stewart in the accents of desperate resolve. Stealthily he beckoned to Mr. West.

"What do you make of this wisdom-loving stunt anyhow?" Stewart demanded of West when the two of them scrambled down the side of the cliff to a sheltered ledge.

"It is like the peace of God, which passeth all understanding," said West in an awesome whisper. "Here, I need another spoonful. What the devil are you doing in this galley anyhow? You're not going to college, you said."

Stewart held the preservative to the light.

"Far from it. On the contrary, I am getting—or trying to get—a liberal education."

"I see. Would it be impertinent to inquire which one?"

"Either," said Stewart sadly. "Could be so happy with either were other dear chappies away. Let's have

another!—But they're like Mary's little lamb, all
four of 'em. Oh, yes; and I'm supposed to be report-
ing the boatraces for my paper—but I wrote 'em up
before I came away so as not to be bothered up here.
Say, I feel better. Let's go back and try him another
fall."

He broke in upon the Idealist rudely.

"Do you mean to tell me that if there were violets—
blue violets—growing on a cliff where no man had
ever been those violets wouldn't be blue?"

The Idealist smiled indulgently. "If there was no
one to see them, certainly there would be no color."

"And no fragrance?"

"Naturally not, there being no one to smell them.
There can be no percipiendum without a percipient.
Let me make it clear to you. The concept of ——"

"Look now!" said Mr. West. "There were two men
on a hillside. There was a sheriff man after them hot-
foot, so they went away. And they left a candle burning in the tent to fool the sheriff person until they
could get a big start on him."

"Hush!" quickly whispered Miss Hoffman, sitting
up very straight. "Let's hear what Mr. Stewart's
friend has to say."

"He's not Stewart's friend—just a friend of Stewart's friend."

Miss Hoffman waved the Pragmatist to silence and
carefully considered Mr. Stewart's friend. This was
the first time she had given Mr. Stewart's friend other
than perfunctory notice. She now atoned for past

neglect. Not bad-looking, Mr. Stewart's friend. He wore a short, pointed, brown beard; he was all dressed in clothes, and up to now he had borne himself unobtrusively.

"Listen!" said Ellinor.

"Well, these men ran away and the sheriff after them. What I want to know is, Did that candle give any light? There were no other men within twenty miles."

Miss Hoffman's face was tinged with a livelier color and Miss Hoffman's eye sparkled discreetly; she listened with a careful attention which bespoke an unusual devotion to metaphysics.

"It gave no light, as I can readily explain to you if you wish. The validity of alleged knowledge cannot ——"

"Oh, no; don't explain. Just tell me. And, no one being there to feel it, the flame gave no heat?"

"That's it."

Mr. West removed his glasses for clearer sight, arched a skeptical eyebrow and twisted his beard with a puzzled air.

"I can't imagine, then," he objected, "how the tent happened to burn up that night. It couldn't have been the candle!"

"Mere sophistry and self-deception," said the Idealist, moved for the first time from his patient tolerance. "You are accustomed to a crude and unverified concept of flame as being necessarily ——"

"Mr. Stewart," called Ellinor, "bring your friend over here, will you? Never mind the sophistry."

"Shall I take Briggs away, too?" inquired Stewart. Briggs was the Pragmatist.

"Oh, no; that will not be necessary," said Ellinor, making room beside her. "I just wanted you to bring your friend to the Senior Singing tomorrow evening, because afterward I want to take him over to the library and read him just one page from my philosopher. I can't talk philosophy, you know, or think it—though you must give me credit for being a fluent listener; but this authority has stated exactly what I feel about such things. I would rather have written that page than any other I have found in literature."

"Why need I bother Stewart? I'm twenty-one," said Mr. West, sinking gracefully into the offered place. "And, just on the chance that I might miss you in the crowd, hadn't I better take you?"

Stewart groaned.

"Another? Come on, Briggs. We're in the way. Let's go make the orator stow his gab and sing Tarpaulin Jacky. Say, when I stop to think of how that word-smith can sing, and what a daisy third baseman he might have made, I feel like killing him."

"And who is this favorite philosopher of yours, Miss Needham?" West asked.

Ellinor laughed.

"You have got us mixed. I am Miss Hoffman. My philosopher? You'd never guess, so I might as well tell you. It's Jerome."

"Saint or William Travers?"

"Neither—Jerome K. Jerome. Goody, they've started the singing! Now the joy begins. No; sit still! Mr. Briggs won't be back. He sings too."

.   .   .   .

Now this is what Miss Hoffman read to Mr. Thomas West on the evening after the boatraces. The line of dots represents—1, boatraces; 2, the long and confidential talk between these two preceding the boatraces; 3, the equally long talk of the next day in and round the quadrangle—before the Senior Singing; and 4, what Stewart and Briggs thought of it all —for Miss Hoffmann and Mr. West had hit it off famously.

"Yes, yes—they are clever and earnest, these shouters; and they have thought and have spoken the thought that was in them, so far as they have understood it, themselves—but what is it all but children teaching children? We are poor little fatherless brats, let to run wild about the streets and alleys of this noisy earth; and the wicked urchins among us play pitch-and-toss or marbles, and fight; and we quiet ones sit on a doorstep and play at school, and little 'Liza Philosophy and Tommy Goodboy will take it in turn to be 'teacher,' and will roar at us, and slap us, and instruct us in all they have learnt. And if we are good and pay attention we shall come to know as much as they—think of that!

213

"Come away—come away from the gutter and the tiresome game. Come away from the din. Come away to the quiet fields, over which the great sky stretches, and where, between us and the stars, there lies but silence; and there in the stillness let us listen to the voice that is speaking within us.

"Hark to it, oh, poor questioning children; it is the voice of God! To the mind of each of us it speaks, showing the light to our longing eyes, making all things clear to us, if we will but follow it. All through the weary days of doubt and terror has it been whispering words of strength and comfort to our aching heart and brain, pointing out the path through the darkness to the knowledge and truth that our souls so hunger for; and all the while we have been straining our ears to catch the silly wisdom of the two-legged human things that cackle round us, and have not heeded it! Let us have done with other men's teaching—other men's guidance. Let us listen to ourselves. ... No; you cannot tell what you have learnt to others. That is what so many are trying to do. They would not understand you and it would only help to swell the foolish din."

"Yes," said Tommy West, a little later, reverting to the eloquent excerpt from Mr. Jerome, "speaking about quiet fields, that's what I'm looking for. I'm going to buy a farm."

"You don't look like a farmer."

"I'm not. That's why I want to farm. Learn something new."

"My grandfather sells farms—down home," said Ellinor meditatively. "If I could help to sell you one he'd give me a fat commission."

"Give me half of it and I'm with you," said Tommy West.

CHAPTER XVIII

AT THE RAINBOW'S END

"Helen's lips are drifting dust;
Ilion is consumed with rust;
All the galleons of Greece
Drink the ocean's dreamless peace;
Lost was Solomon's purple show
Restless centuries ago;
Stately empires wax and wane—
Babylon, Barbary and Spain—
Only one thing, undefaced,
Lasts, though all the worlds lie waste
And the heavens are overturned,
—Dear, how long ago we learned!"
    FREDERICK LAWRENCE KNOWLES

"WHAT I don't see," said Ellinor, "is why you stay here if you're not satisfied. I wouldn't. Nothing pleases you. You're always finding fault. And lazy! Tommy West, I do believe you're the laziest person I ever knew, and I've known lots of lazy ones!"

Tommy dipped his paddle languidly, both to dis-

216

prove the last statement and to keep the canoe to its drifting course, clear of the eel-grass. He settled back with a little sigh, plainly too indolent to refute the accusation.

Ellinor was curled up daintily on a pile of cushions, sunburned and sunny-eyed. Tommy's sleeves were rolled back to show his sunburned arms. Owecum was near Ithaca. Owecum rather followed the Cornell manner, and Tommy West was doing new Roman deeds every day. He called them "stunts."

Ellinor returned to the attack, seeing that Tommy —the Mr. West stage had been passed long ago—was not to be moved from his lotus-lily content by any halfway measures.

"You grumble at so many things—rain, house-plants and fancy cooking, embroidery work, automobiles, motorcycles ——"

"But I like out-of-doors—and sunshine—and running water—and canoes—and waterboats," said Tommy drowsily. "Lots o' little things I care about."

"You don't like bridge"—Tommy opened his mouth to retort, but thought better of it—"or golf, or tennis."

"Baseball," said Tommy, economical of energy.

"Yes; you do manage to get up an enthusism for baseball. So far as I know that's the only thing you really care about in all New York." Tommy regarded Miss Ellinor in pained amazement. "You don't like churches ——"

Tommy sat up.

217

"Come, I say now! There's nothing I like better than a good view of an old church, with trees all round it and just the spires to be seen above them—bells pealing out over the water, 'way off. Why, it sounds as good as an alarm clock when some other man's off to catch a train."

"You don't like doctors, and poor Roy Delancey" —here Tommy scowled so sternly that his glasses fell off—"and lawyers, and ——"

"Automobiles again?" suggested Tommy.

"There! You see! You dislike so many more things than you like. You've come to the end of your list."

"The things I like, I like so much more than the things I don't like.

"Naturally."

"I mean, I like what I like so much more than I dislike what I don't like. You know very well what I mean. There's that gloom donkey, Delancey, now. I don't dislike him so much—only when he's round underfoot. On the other hand ——"

"And you don't like the hills," said Ellinor hurriedly.

"Oh, but you are all wrong there. I do. Only not afoot. It's just going up and down I don't like—especially up."

"Why don't you drive then?"

Tommy sighed.

"My farmer won't let me have my team. I got another good horse for myself, but it didn't do any good.

He hired a boy and used him to cultivate potatoes—the horse, you know, not the boy. If I get another it would be just the same. Of course, there's my saddle horse; but he won't work, thank goodness! I took care of that. That man works all the time. First, it was planting buckwheat ——"

"Sowing. Oh, Tommy! You'll never be a farmer."

"Sowing buckwheat—then cutting the rye; then the oats; and working in the potatoes all the time. And now he's talking about doing fall plowing until it's time to dig potatoes. Why can't he plow next spring? I want to know. I never saw such a man. He gets up at four o'clock, I guess, and works until eight. I don't want him to do fall plowing. He ought to rest two or three months after harvest. I go out and try to talk to him, but it just makes him cross. You'd think he'd be glad to stop!"

"It's your silly prattle about farming. You make him nervous. He told me about it. 'Miss Ellinor,' he said, 'it doesn't seem possible that any man could know so little about so many things as Mr. West does, and be alive!' Tommy, I believe you do it on purpose, just to bedevil him. You ought to be ashamed."

Tommy stroked his little pointed beard to smooth away a guilty grin.

"It does annoy him," he admitted.

"And his wife complains that you're all the time trying to talk her into doing her washing on Wednesday and ironing on Friday. Why did you come here anyhow? You don't like New York."

219

Tommy pondered on this, the canoe turned broadside on.

"Baseball?" he hazarded, brightening. "I'm just daffy about baseball." The canoe drifted slowly downstream, now stern-end first.

"Tommy West, turn this boat round!"

"View's just as good this way," grumbled Tommy with admiring eyes.

"You turn this boat round and answer my question. I can understand why you would visit the East— every one likes to travel; but why did you buy that farm? You wouldn't learn farming in a thousand years! And I'm sure grandfather cheated you on it scandalously."

Tommy stared hopelessly up at his farm, which marched with the Hoffman homestead. The Hoffman pasture lay along the high, steep hillside polka-dotted with prosperous Holsteins. Above, crowning the long hill, was Tommy's property—not yet the West place. It would not be that for fifty years to come. Owecum was conservative. It was still the Barton place, though the Barton who once owned it had lived in the city of New York since the early eighties. From the Barton farm a modern cannon would carry to the birthplace of our most noted American financier. Unfortunately it was neglected until too late.

A house on a hill cannot be hid, but this one gave only a few white glimpses through the long double row of maples. The big red barn stood out against the sky-line, which made it seem longer, if possible, than it really was; its situation, the tall, round silo and the clear river below combined to give a castled-crag-of-Drachenfels effect.

Mr. West regarded his property with a puzzled air.

"The maples, maybe?"

"Tommy West! As if any one ever bought a farm for the maples!"

Tommy West readjusted his eyeglasses and took a longer look. "Oh, I know! It's the view!" he announced triumphantly. "Do you know, I often think to myself that if I just had this country out in Idaho I'd be awfully proud of it! I'd swell up my chest and show it to you Eastern folks as proud as if I made it. From my place I certainly have a fine view. And I got one-fourth of the commission, remember."

It was a beautiful view. From that eminence the eye took in the long reaches of a noble river from Mudjekeewis Island to Ivanhoe—a river that Tommy West with characteristic perversity called the Senator-hanna; the white town nestled in dense greenery, the distant spires so dear to Tommy's heart thrust up above the fine old trees; northward, the long waves of low hills dimmed to a level haze toward Ithaca.

"Funny why they don't name any of these hills," said Mr. West.

"Why don't you name yours then?" Miss Ellinor by no means considered the view an adequate reason for the purchase of that farm, but she did not push the query farther, having a faint surmise of her own.

"I will," said Tommy promptly. "I'll call it Mount

221

Helena—after your cousin. She's been mighty nice to me."

"Haven't I been good to you too?"

"Oh, you're good to everybody," said Tommy.

The ambiguity of the compliment was not lost on Ellinor. Mr. West, so far as intent goes, was a monopolist; and, when thwarted, he was inclined to be huffy, not to say sulky. Miss Ellinor smiled her sweetest; she declaimed with airy benignity:

> "If you have a friend worth loving—
>   Love him! Yes, and let him know
> That you love him ere life's evening
>   Tinge his brow with sunset glow."

As she proclaimed these liberal sentiments, she was pleased to observe that the glow which tinged Tommy's brow was an angry one.

"I think you might have named it for me," she pouted. "My name is almost exactly the same as hers."

"Your name doesn't abbreviate so aptly as hers though. We can call it Mount Lena for short, coming down."

"My name can be shortened too," said Ellinor.

"There's no 'H' in it. No—no; your name's exactly right just as it is. I never knew a name to fit so well," said Tommy enthusiastically. In his animation and delight he even took a stroke or two with his paddle.

Ellinor caught the obscure reference, for Tommy had showed her the lines concerning her Christian name, after an unusually severe grilling. Clearly it was time to put Mr. West in his place.

"There'll be a party of young folks out for tennis this afternoon. You'll stay, won't you?"

"Who is it?" Tommy eyed her with suspicion. "That ass Delancey, of course. Who else?"

"Mr. Freeman and Esther, and the two philosophers, and Mr. Stewart—if he can get away."

"Same old gang. It seems to me," said Mr. West morosely, "there are a good many men in the party."

"Is there any particular girl you want to come?"

"Oh, you know what I mean! You ought to have more girls. I don't get to see you at all."

"The young ladies hardly care to come 'way out here. It would look," said Ellinor primly, "as though they were coming to meet the young men."

"Esther comes though! In Idaho——"

"Oh, Esther—that's different!" said Ellinor. "She comes to see Freeman!" She reverted to her original query, conscious that her solution would not bear analysis. "If you like Idaho so well, why did you ever come here?"

"I can't just explain the charm of—Idaho. You'd have to see it for yourself. Why, you know, you said you liked New Mexico so well when you were down there last summer ——"

"Last winter and spring. We got back here two months before you came. Yes; it was wonderful. I'm going back there too."

Mr. West took up his paddle again. He looked cross.

"You liked the people there?"

Miss Ellinor's rare dimple appeared.

"They were delightful—some of them."

Mr. West sent the startled Water Witch on her way with a dozen agitated strokes. It was a devious way. Mr. West was not nautical.

"I see you get letters from there," said Tommy with a meaning glance at the pocket of her jacket, where it lay beside the picture hat.

"Oh yes! That's from Billy. I had forgotten. I brought that along to read you an extract from a note written to him by a Mexican boy he was helping with his English. Here—you read it yourself." She tossed him the envelope.

Tommy hesitated.

"Other people's letters—now ——"

"Oh, nonsense! You need only read the note from the Mexican boy."

So Tommy read it while the canoe boxed the compass.

"I received very littel letter from you, and you will know that I do not like many to no received letter from you; but I believe that you when to receipt this letter I believed that do you will to do more lest.

"Now I will teld you a littel on the *conversación* that we has in your country; he said to me that when you was in this moderate—*contenido*—country, alone them will be able the innocence that them are enjoymen."

"You can read the other if you want to. It's only Billy White."

"Friend of yours?" His brow clouded.

"Silly! Of course he is! Is it likely I'd write to him if he wasn't a friend?"

"And that other fellow—the big thick letters—is he a friend too?" Storms, hurricanes and great local disturbances!

"Oh—him?"

Her hand trailed in the water; she watched it with intent interest.

"Billy White's a nice boy, Tommy; but this other—Tommy, he's just wonderful! an out-of-doors man too. You'd like him, I'm sure."

From the expression of Tommy's face this may be doubted. If a gentleman may scowl at a lady Tommy scowled.

After a troubled silence the girl went on, still watching the hand in the water.

"I've never seen any one like him. . . . Maybe I'll tell you about him—sometime. He's very poor; but—as the Griffin said of the Minor Canon—'he was brave and good and honest, and I think I should have relished him.' " There was a catch in her voice. "I think, perhaps, if he hadn't been poor—or if I was poor ——" The words died away. Tears stood in her eyes when she looked up. "Take me home, Tommy! I'm a wicked, ungrateful girl, and I ought to be ashamed to talk about him like this—to you."

Tommy was nothing loath to go. He was consumed

225

with jealousy and anger, which made him, as canoeist, more awkward than ever. He shut his teeth together until the Vandyke thrust out aggressively; he dipped the paddle with savage energy. Miss Ellinor huddled silent in the bow—and poor Tommy West saw that she trembled.

"The ignorant ruffian! Battered bully! Little better than a desperado!" Tommy did not say it aloud, but he half formed the words behind his clenched teeth as the girl's shaking form became quiet. "By Heaven, he shan't have her!"

A slight inkling of his own absurdity must have reached Tommy's troubled mind, for he grinned once; but the grin did not last.

The poor little Water Witch made a bad voyage. If an eel had been towed in her stern, infallibly it would have broken its back.

The girl sat up presently. Her face was flushed and her eyelids were red, but she made a brave effort for composure and attempted a desultory conversation to which Tommy contributed gruff monosyllables. She gave him her hand as he steadied her for the landing. Tommy felt, or thought he felt, a distinct pressure— thought so the more for the grateful and confidential glance that accompanied it; and poor Tommy's heart bounded joyously. At least, she trusted him; she was striving to overcome this disastrous weakness. Had she not said that she would tell about that—that disreputable scoundrel—some day? Did she mean—

what else could she mean? Tommy's feet scarcely touched the ground.

His elation was doomed to be shortlived however. As they neared the Hoffman home Ellinor walked more rapidly—and Tommy was disgusted to see that the R.F.D. man was approaching from the other side. His face turned fairly livid with wrath and pain. So that was why she wanted to come back so suddenly!

His worst fears were confirmed. There was a big, thick letter for Ellinor; her hand slipped so that he saw the New Mexico postmark and the bold handwriting of the address. With a murmured apology and a shy, sidelong, drooping glance for Tommy as she passed him, Ellinor ran up the steps with joyous feet.

There was a letter for Tommy too. The postman left Tommy's mail at Hoffman's now as a regular thing; always with a discreet query as to the progress of Tommy's farming.

Tommy needed so much agricultural information from Ellinor's grandfather that he had a sunny south room of his own in the rambling, quaint, old-fashioned house. He trudged heavily to his room now, weighing the letter indignantly in his hand as he went. "Why a girl like Ellinor would throw herself away on a sorry adventurer like that, I can't see!" he muttered.

There were three inclosures. Two of them were brief scrawls from Ed Dowlin and Johnny Dines. He threw them by unread and tore open the fat letter for Mr. Jeff Bransford, Escondido, New Mexico.

"She doesn't hurt herself writing very often!" Jeff grumbled.

Mr. West's face grew less cloudy, fair, and at last positively sunny as he hurried over the pages. She was more than merely grateful to Jeff—that was beyond doubt. He began to purr; but near the last he came to what gave him pause—I had nearly written claws.

"Our new neighbor, Mr. West—I told you about him, didn't I?—is down here a great deal. My grandfather sells farms on commission. He sold this one to Mr. West and I'm afraid he made him pay far too much for it. Mr. West is a very nice man, but he's no farmer. He is down here a great deal to get advice about his farming operations. Mother likes him very much. Father would too, I suppose, but he's away on business now.

"I told mother about you, Jeff—a little. She thinks it was noble of you, of course—but you know how mothers are. Naturally she was anxious. She doesn't know you, you see. She told me she thought it would be as well if I didn't say anything to father yet. I guess she thinks I'll forget you if she gives me time enough. As if I could do that, Jeff!

"Yes, I knew Mr. Griffith and his three friends; but there was no Gibson in Arcadia that I remember now. There were lots of transients, you know. You didn't tell me much about Mr. Gibson; or, in fact, about anything after you got away from Double Mountain. Tell me next time you write.

"Billy writes to me once in a while. He wrote me pages on pages about some of your past exploits. You'll have to quiet down, sir—when you get rich! Some one told him a lot of the stories were lies; but, says Billy, 'I'd like to be the kind of man they tell such lies about!' He admires you very much, Jeff. So does Rex Griffith—not to mention your little friend. Did I tell you that Mr. West bought the farm adjoining ours? It's not very fertile, but it's a delightful old house. He took us up there yesterday. He's quite wealthy, I think."

The reading paused for bitter comment:

"Oh, damn Mr. West! What do I care about him and his money? I'd like to see him in some of the tights I've been in! It's mighty funny she never said anything about him before. In all the letters I've had from her since I come, not one twitter about Mr. West! She says a plenty about him now. It's a wonder she takes time to write at all!"

He turned back to the letter.

"I hate to think of you out there working so hard, Jeff. It seems a shame for a man of your ability to wear his life away for no reward. You said you were going to get rich, you know—for me! You'll never get rich there. Do you know how old I am? Of course you don't. You don't know anything about me, really— just that I treated you very badly. Don't think I am a wicked, mercenary girl, dear. You mustn't. Money is

229

a good thing, but there are better things—laughter and joy, and—love, Jeff!

"I wish you could be up here now; not only because I want to see you so badly—you know I do, Jeff—but because everything is so beautiful. Oh, boy, your country is grand, wonderful—everything that is big and clean and young, and all that; but there is nothing in New Mexico more beautiful than New York in summer—or springtime, which is best of all! It's horrible here in winter though. One ought to have two homes—cut the year in halves. Are the years long for you, Jeff?

"We have been having all sorts of dissipation—automobiling, canoeing, tennis, dances. Two aeroplanes flew by—or, rather, one flew by and the other stopped here. And the Owecum boys have a really good ball team—all local talent except for a few Cornell boys through the vacation. They play twice a week and they beat all comers—nearly. We never miss a game. You said in your last letter that you were a 'fan'; so I thought I'd tell you. Isn't it funny? I don't know anything about what you like—except me!

"Mr. West does too—likes baseball, I mean; not little me. He doesn't care for autos at all; but, of course, he goes along. He likes horseback riding better and so do I—though scarcely any one rides here. I used to ride so much in California—constantly, in fact. We go for a ride almost every fine day. Papa has just bought a new car. The one we have here—the old one—is pretty badly dilapidated. Mr. West says it has the heaves and a bone-spavin. He is from the West too —from Idaho.

"And now, my poor old hard-working boy, I really must stop. I've promised to go canoeing tonight by moonlight. You've no idea how beautiful the river is. And we sing. Mr. West has a very nice voice—not strong, but very clear and expressive. He puts so much meaning into it. And he knows a lot of the most extraordinary songs. Do you remember our song—Jamie?

"Here is part of an old song my mother taught me —Jamie. When you lie down to sleep tonight—the night you read this, I mean—under your great warm stars, think I am singing it to you, and sleep—and dream of me.

" 'Poor weary hands, that all the day
    Were set to labor hard and long,
At last we reach the close of day—
    The time has come for evensong.
Tonight forget the stormy strife
    And know what Heaven shall send is best.
Lay down the tangled web of life—
    'Tis time for rest—'tis time for rest!'

"Good night, boy!
    "Your little friend,   Ellinor."

"P. S. Speaking of stars, we had a comet party the other night at the Hoffman house—that sounds like a hotel, doesn't it? People have called it that so long we scarcely notice it any more—because of the alliteration, I fancy. It was very exclusive. Just Mr. Freeman

231

and his Esther, and our new neighbor and little me. Mr. West said if he had known astronomy was such a fascinating study he would have taken it up long ago."

The new neighbor almost tore the letter in two in his exasperation. This was too much! They had not seen the comet once—or looked for it. Freeman and Esther had the music room; he remembered that Freeman would play the flute, no matter if he woke every one in the house. Ellinor and he had kept the cozy corner for themselves. He was fairly aflame with jealousy and anger.

"By Heaven! I believe she's falling in love with him! Half her letter is about him. This is pretty reading now, for a tired man riding sixty miles across the desert from South Rainbow to get a letter from her—working his fool head off for her! Nice state of affairs, this is! Him and his money!" He glanced at his watch, fuming. "Now she won't be down until dinnertime, I know! She'll sit right down and write to him. Hasn't the girl any pride? Here she keeps two sets of crossed letters going all the time—sometimes three sets—for all the world like a juggler tossing balls at a fair. She might at least have decency enough to wait until she gets his answer to her last letter." A stanhope drove into the yard. "Here comes that gloomy ass, Delancey! Pity he couldn't wait and come when the others do. One consolation—he won't see Ellinor now. She won't stir until she writes a letter to that poor pitiful fool! Uncouth barbarian!" He surveyed Delancey through the window maliciously and brightened at the sight. "It's a good wind that blows nobody ill. I'm not going down to talk to him—gloomy ass! Let Grandpa Hoffman entertain him. I might as well sit down and write to Ellinor so as to send it when the postman goes back."

Which he did. His pen fairly flew. The sorrows and fears and hopes and mishaps of Mr. Jeff Bransford, as there set down, would melt the heart of a stone. There were bitter allusions to Mr. West, too, and slighting surmises. Mr. Bransford was maddened by fear and jealousy.

After the midday meal—which with no unworthy evasion was dinner, the Hoffmans being farming folk —Delancey the interloper sat with Ellinor on the big porch, leaving Tommy with Mrs. Hoffman. That gentle lady was surprised to find Mr. West's wonted deference just a little forced—one might almost say reluctant.

Altogether he passed a wretched afternoon. The tennis players appeared at three in a crowded motor. Ellinor and Stewart—of course he found time to come —were matched against Freeman and a philosopher —the Idealist. Miss Esther, as referee, sat in the car with Tommy and found him dull and grumpy—not even sarcastic. He was very miserable, but he obtained a ray of comfort by observing the empiric philosopher entertaining the gloomy ass.

Miss Esther wearied of her moody cavalier at last and left him to nurse his grouch while she went to exercise her duties at the net—on Freeman's side.

Tommy was drafted for the next match, despite his sulky protest. Tommy played very badly; the gloomy ass, who was his partner, played even worse, though usually rather a dab; and they were beaten ignominiously by Miss Esther and the Empiricist. Spirited recriminations ensued, for meantime the Idealist was talking philosophy to Ellinor, and it was hard to tell which of the beaten partners was the gloomier.

Tea was served on the great old colonial porch. Then in the music room as the dusk came on some one started Cayuga Waters. It is a good song. There was silence afterward. It was broken by Stewart:

"Won't you sing Dearie for me, Miss Ellinor?" His punctuation was peculiar and not that recorded above; it roused the spirit of emulation.

Up rose then the gloomy ass, who was feeling decidedly better since tea.

"Won't you sing my song first—our song, Ellinor?" The unhappy young voice shook with its pleading.

"It would gratify me very much."

Thus far, in concert, the two philosophers. They paused and scowled at each other, mutually disconcerted at the ill-timed impertinence, and simultaneously they fell back upon direct speech. "Sing my song, please!" they chanted in chorus.

"Ellinor!" said poor Delancey.

Under drooped lids she shot a swift glance at Tommy. Tommy glared in gloomy dignity.

"Oh, yes; sing my song, too, by all means," Tommy said bitterly. "Make it unanimous!"

So Ellinor went to the piano; she turned her face to the west, a little pale—and she sang about Jamie!

There were tears in her voice—yes, in her eyes! Tommy's blood reeled; his throat ached with love and longing and wrath. This was too much—too hard to bear! While Miss Esther sang, in turn, Tommy quietly left the room, wandered disconsolately through the trembling dusk and kicked the car. This was too emphatically much!

"Faithless! Oh, she promised! But Sandy has money—that's the main thing! . . . And that look she gave me before she sang . . . Plain treachery—that's what it is! . . . 'Your little friend,' indeed! And then to look at any man like that! . . . This thing has got to be settled. His little friend! I'll see about that!"

.   .   .   .

Young Roy Delancey went early—that had not been his song. When the car had whirled away—when the last shout of joyous laughter had died—Mr. Tommy West turned to Ellinor.

"Will you come to the music room with me, Ellinor?"

"Why, certainly!" She led the way, "Poor Tommy! Did it have the doldrums? Do you want me to sing for you now—just you, Tommy?"

235

"I want you to live for me—just me!" said Tommy hoarsely.

"Mr. West!"

"Ellinor! Give me a chance! I will wait. I will be patient. You must have seen how it was with me, Ellinor. Can't you try to love me—just a little?"

"Oh, Tommy! A little? Yes, a great deal! I think it is you who have been blind. There has never been any one else, Tommy. It was you from the first."

She gave him her hands; she trembled to him—his lips brushed hers. . . . Then he stepped back as though the touch had burned him.

"Oh, woman!" Tommy moaned, aghast at her unshrinking duplicity. "Oh, woman!"

"You talk like a Latin grammar, Tommy! What's the matter?" She caught the tragic despair of his face and drew back in alarm. "What is the matter?"

"Infamous!" he burst out. "Faithless! Perfidious wretch!"

"Fine manners these! Are you mad?" She threw herself into a chair and buried her face, trembling with emotion.

"I brought you 'honor and faith and a sure intent,' " said Tommy sternly. "I trusted you, Ellinor! I will never trust a woman again!"

"And this is my hoped-for happiness! Here's a lover for you!" wailed the bewildered girl. "Go, sir! Go! No—wait! I must give you back your present."

"I never gave you a present—some other man

doubtless!" said Tommy with bitter and cutting scorn. "You should be more careful."

The girl's shoulders heaved at this insult.

"Look the other way, sir! Turn your head! You shall have your present and then you may go if you wish."

Confused and bewildered, Tommy obeyed her.

"Miss Hoffman, I never gave you a present in my life!" he protested.

"You did!" sobbed Ellinor. "You said when you gave it to me you hoped it would bring me good luck."

"I? I?" stammered Tommy. "I never even gave you so much as a book."

She sprang to her feet. She was laughing, blushing, glowing. In her hand was the little gold chain.

"Hold out your hand, sir!"

Tommy's mind was whirling; he obeyed. She laid a little gold locket in his palm. It was warm, that little locket.

"I never saw this locket before in all my life!" gasped Tommy.

"Open it!"

He opened it: the little eohippus glared up at him!

"Ellinor!—Charley Gibson!"

"Tommy!—Tobe!—Jeff!—Jamie!" said Ellinor.

The little eohippus stared unwinking from the floor.

(THE BEGINNING)